Autumn Lightning

Autumn Lightning
The Education of an American Samurai

Dave Lowry

Foreword by Daniel Furuya

 Shambhala   *Boston & London*   1985

SHAMBHALA PUBLICATIONS, INC.
314 Dartmouth Street
Boston, Massachusetts 02116

SHAMBHALA PUBLICATIONS, INC.
at Routledge & Kegan Paul
14 Leicester Square
London WC2H 7PH

First Edition
Printed in the United States of America
Distributed in the United States by Random House
and in Canada by Random House of Canada Ltd.

Library of Congress Cataloging in Publication Data
Lowry, David.
    Autumn lightning.
    1. Lowry, David.   2. Swordsmen—United States—
Biography.   3. Swordplay—Japan.   4. Samurai.
I. Title
GV1144.2.L68A32   1985   796.8'6   84-23562
ISBN 0-87773-305-8 (pbk.)
ISBN 0-394-73027-5 (Random House: pbk.)

For my parents, who showed me the dream,
and for my Sensei, who showed me the Way.

Contents

Foreword

The bamboo survives due to its resiliency. It can bend with the force of the wind and the weight of the snow because its roots grow deep and strong. The roots of Budo, the traditional Japanese martial arts, go back over a thousand years. But, in modern times, many of these roots have been cut, transplanted to other countries, or trampled upon by the march of time in their own homeland. To survive, Budo has changed and adapted itself to its new environment considerably. We must, however, always be mindful that by straying too far away from the original nature of Budo, we may be in danger of losing its essence. Change is the law of nature. But we must never forget that, in the face of the adverse winds of time, the resiliency of Budo, like that of the bamboo, depends on the strength and depth of its roots.

As a student of martial arts for many years, I fear we may be losing these roots altogether. Indeed, we may be sacrificing the tree for the fruit and achieving only a temporary gain. It is with great pleasure then that I note that devoted students and scholars of the martial arts such as Dave Lowry are making great efforts to recultivate these roots for the benefit of all. Mr. Lowry has undertaken two difficult projects: recounting his own personal experiences in martial arts training under a traditional teacher, and relating the development of the Yagyu Shinkage ryu, an outstanding school of traditional Japanese swordsmanship. I hope this unique approach will bring deep insight into the martial arts for all interested students.

Daniel Furuya

(Daniel Furuya, an aikido teacher in Los Angeles, California, is a leading authority on the culture of feudal Japan, with a particular interest in the classical martial arts of that country and in the swordsmanship of the Yagyu school of fencing. Furuya Sensei is at the fourth *dan* in *hombu* aikido and at the second *dan* in the Muso Shinden ryu of iaido.)

Preface

When I began to plan this book I knew that a good deal of material would need to be translated because there has been almost no serious literature written in English on the classical martial arts of Japan. For help, I went to a young Japanese man who had immigrated to the United States a few years ago and was lecturing on Oriental philosophy and teaching Zen at a nearby college. Our conversation on Zen was rambling, punctuated by long, companionable silences. Finally, I got around to telling him of my problem. Many of the older treatises I was using for research were couched in archaic Japanese, so if I stumbled during my efforts at translating them, I wanted to count on his assistance. He readily agreed and we talked on, discussing some of the difficulties of rendering ideas from one language into another. After a prolonged pause, he asked me why I practiced *kenjutsu*, the techniques of wielding the Japanese sword. Because Zen and swordsmanship have had a lengthy and intimate relationship in Japan, I was surprised at the question. I started to explain how a study of the art led to improvement in physical and mental capabilities, but the Zen man interrupted. "No," he said firmly. "Kenjutsu is only killing with the sword."

As attitudes and institutions progress so rapidly in our world, we risk becoming further alienated from previous generations. Even among the Japanese, it seems, appreciation of the traditional arts of the samurai is waning. I cannot speak for the whole of those who are still devoted to these arts, nor can I even speak from the perspective of a Japanese. Yet it is worthwhile, I think, to present modern society a personal account of an education in swordsmanship and the other classical arts of the samurai, revealing them as endeavors more meaningful in purpose and with deeper ends than just killing. From the experience, as I hope is found in these pages, they are indeed, very much more.

Naturally, whenever anyone devotes time to a particular discipline, he acquires knowledge and insights that give him a wider perception of it. My involvement with the martial crafts of feudal Japan has extended for over half my life. In an effort to put the events of those years into a sort of readable order, I have altered time and characters and places a bit. For that reason, I must say that while the contents of this book aren't all factual, they are all true—embarrassingly so at times, for me. Additionally, I have ascribed conversations and personal details to historical characters to make their stories more understandable, but all of those individuals did exist and contribute to the development of the Yagyu Shinkage ryu, and their actions, as I've recorded them, are a matter of fact.

I must thank some of the people who encouraged me to undertake this project. From Japan: Watatani Kiyoshi, that country's foremost scholar of feudal history; Otsubo Shiho Sensei, one of the remaining masters of the Yagyu school of the sword; and his daughter, Haruko, all provided me with appreciated information, as did the offices of the Nara prefectural government. The late Donn Draeger prodded and cajoled when I needed it. In this country, I was given invaluable advice by my friends Randall

Hassell and Daniel Furuya, and I hope sincerely that my efforts have been equal to the expectations of all of them.

Thanks to the Quincy College Library of Quincy, Illinois. Their outstanding Asian Collection provided invaluable help in research and translation. I believe the staff there considered me something of a ghost, appearing once a month mysteriously to haunt the stacks, but they left me alone and the hours I spent there were as pleasant as they were productive.

Also, to the *uchi no yatsu*, who knows little of Yagyu *heiho*, but who knows much about the ways of a Yagyunin.

Excerpts from *The Shino Suite*, by Ronald Tanaka, and *Shibumi*, by Trevanian, are used with the kind permission of the authors.

i've been taught to expect a certain precision
in human relationships. in aesthetic terms,
this means that one can't expect to have both
beauty and comfort. i assume you understand.

Ronald Tanaka, *The Shino Suite*

1.

Meeting with the Past

Surrounded by the pines that closed in his yard, the swordsman crouched motionless. His gray kimono and black, skirt-like *hakama* grew damp in the predawn mist, but his attention was focused on the drops of water that collected first on a branch above his head, then dripped to the ground with noiseless regularity. He seemed to be waiting for a particular drop, his expression reflecting a profound patience. The bead of water finally fell, and with perfect celerity, his right hand tore the samurai sword from its scabbard at his side. Still kneeling, he slashed a wide arc in the heavy, wet air, stopping the weapon as abruptly as if it had struck some invisible barrier. Then slowly, methodically, he pulled a cloth from a fold in his kimono and wiped moisture from the blade's surface, for he had cut through the descending drop, shattering it into smaller droplets that sparkled on the steel like diamonds in the morning's new light.

While the swordsman continued the solitary exercises with his weapon, I wriggled farther under the handquilted covers my great-grandmother had patched together, burrowing to find a few more minutes of sleep.

Get your motor runnin'
Head out on the highway
Lookin' for adventure
And whatever comes our way
Born to be wild . . .

The music swelling from the alarm clock-radio by my head promised a heady freedom in that early autumn of 1968, but the blasting noise was also a reminder that I had to get up and get ready for another day of junior high school.

Nothing in the morning indicated that the day would be different. On the long bus ride ahead, I would have to fabricate a believable excuse for not finishing a math assignment, already two days overdue. I would have to sit through eight hours of uninspired attempts at educating myself, hurry home afterward to stuff the bulky jacket and pants of a judo uniform into a bag, and then be off to practice at the state university gym. For a thirteen-year-old boy of the Midwest, it wasn't a day—or a life, for that matter—too much out of the ordinary at all. In those days, judo was an unlikely sport for a Missouri boy, but my adolescent passion might just as easily have been loosed upon cars, or stamp collecting, or girls. As it happened, I had always had interests both in things Japanese and in the avoidance of getting beaten up, so three evenings of my weeks were taken with the art of judo, learning how to fall and how to make my classmates at the gym fall.

In fact, what had been the only disruption in my life that year was becoming so much a routine that I hardly considered it outstanding anymore. Walking to judo practice, I would take a detour down a street near the university, where many of the professors lived. It was a street of monstrous old houses with towering ceilings and three, or even four, stories, a street where sounds much louder than the strains of Bach or Vivaldi were hushed by oaks and

4

pines and maples, as impressive in size as were the houses beside them. I walked along the quiet street until I came to a house nearly hidden by trees, with a front yard full of iris and lily beds that probably never saw the sun until all the trees around them were bare of leaves.

This was the house where a Japanese guy lived, as my judo friends had heard it, who was supposed to be an expert in swordfighting. While we were all intrigued by the idea of a modern day samurai living in the middle of the Ozarks, I was the only one persistent and impudent enough to find out more. I did it by going to the front door, knocking, and telling the Oriental woman who answered that I had come to learn swordsmanship. What I noticed immediately about her appearance was that, even though she looked to be well into her fifties, her skin was creamy, like weathered ivory, and she had the most wonderfully slitted eyes.

"You must have the wrong address," she said. "There is no one here who teaches fighting with a sword."

That's not exactly the way it sounded. Her accent made the words come out, "You mus hava wrongu address. Dare isa noone here who teacha fighting wisa sword," and her voice stayed in the air between us, the way a note played on a fine piano will hang on and on if it's struck in the center of a big, empty room. I think I might have kept coming back to that house, just to hear her voice. It was that pleasant. But from my reading I also knew it was a custom in old Japan for prospective fencing students to be forced to beg for instruction several times to insure their sincerity. So to listen to a voice that continued on even after the words were finished, to see if she knew something about "fighting wisa sword" that she wasn't telling me, and to prove I was as stubborn as any Japanese pupil might have been, I came back. Three nights a week I went to her door to ask the same question and, without a trace of annoyance or amusement, the woman assured me that no one there taught fencing. I would nod and be on my way to judo practice. In nearly a month's worth of visits the only clue I had that I wasn't at the "wrongu address" was that she hadn't yet called the authorities to come and haul me away. It was not the most encouraging of consolations.

Just when our thrice-weekly exchanges had grown into a pleasant sort of game that I was beginning to expect to last into the following spring and beyond, they stopped without the slightest notice. I was still trying to sleep through the radio's morning nagging—failing as usual; and still presenting novel excuses for not completing my homework—failing as usual. And, as usual, I stopped by the house on the quiet street to ask the woman with the creamy skin to teach me how to use a sword. This time, I succeeded. Well, partially anyway.

"You come back a tomorrow," she said, her voice lingering in that delightful way. "Mebbe dar be someone who can herp you."

A change in the scheme of things it certainly was. As it turned out, I had no idea what a change it was going to be.

To the average Occidental, the Japanese martial arts are most often thought of in terms of *judo, karate-do,* and *aikido.* That's an understandable connotation, for those methods of combat are the ones most successfully transplanted from their Asian homeland. Collectively, they are known there as the *budo*, a Japanese word meaning literally "martial ways," and indicating that judo, karatedo, and aikido are spiritual paths for approaching a particular way of life. The originators of the budo intended for them to be means of physical and self-defense training, of course, but also, and more importantly, the martial ways were meant to instill moral values in a practitioner, improve his personality, and make him an asset to society. Because of the insistence upon morality and virtue, these budo have produced some of the greatest thinkers and political leaders in the history of Japan, and they are often considered by the Japanese to be the bright, *yang* side of the country's martial spirit. If they are, then by the tenets of Oriental philosophy, there must also be a darker, *yin* side. Surely this facet of yin is revealed in the nature of the *bugei*.

The bugei are the traditional martial arts of the samurai (as distinguished from the more recently created budo, or martial *ways*), rarely practiced anymore in modern-day Japan and almost completely unheard of outside of it. Superficially, they might look alike, but the budo and bugei are really quite different. The former are pretty much limited in scope to judo, aikido, karatedo, *kendo* (fencing with bamboo staves), and *kyudo* (archery). The bugei, on the other hand, represent a startlingly wide diversity. Almost a limitless array of techniques were codified into bugei, or "military arts," as that word can be translated. *Hojutsu*, for instance, is the art of binding an enemy with a short cord. *Sueijutsu* is the art of swimming and treading water while clad in the light wooden armor once worn by the samurai. Spitting needles into an opponent's eye (*fukumijutsu*), methods of deflecting flying arrows from his bow (*yadomejutsu*), even hypnotizing him into defeat (*saiminjutsu*)—all were crafts familiar to the feudal warriors of Japan, but as woodblock prints of that era still show, the samurai's favorite art was in the handling of his long, two-handed sword, by ways he referred to as *kenjutsu*, the techniques of the blade.

All of this was explained to me the next day as I sat at attention, eager and uncomfortably erect in the living room of the house on the quiet street. The man doing the talking was Japanese, slightly built except for the heavily muscled forearms he folded across his chest. In a polo shirt and slacks, he didn't look like my idea of a fierce samurai, but even when relaxed, his posture had a formidable bearing about it, as if he were capable of commanding respect by his bodily presence alone. Clearly, he was as old as the woman I'd met so often at the front door, yet just as clearly, he was not a man you could ever slap on the back and call "Pops." No way.

Without speaking further for a moment, he poured the steaming contents of a teapot into two cups on the table between us, and I took in the surroundings. The inside of the house was of a style I have to label as Gothic. I don't know a more apt description for the sort of place that has a minor maze of rooms and hallways and alcoves—so many that you wonder if the house isn't so much inhabited, as it is gradually explored. In the living room, braided rugs protected the floor's dark finish from the furniture: a plump sofa and overstuffed chairs that all looked to be as comfortable as the one I was in (even ramrod straight, as I was, it's hard to sit *on* furniture like that). There were high bookshelves, and windows even higher, a couple of them opaque with stained glass designs. To my right yawned an enormous fireplace that could have accommodated more logs than a man might carry in both arms. Only a couple of wispy ink paintings displaying brushed calligraphy, and the books on the shelves, titled in indecipherable Japanese characters, distinguished the room from any other of similar architecture and decor.

My host handed me a cup of tea and watched while I took a sip, trying not to grimace at its green bitterness. "Being a *bugeisha*, a pupil of the bugei, is not something you . . . " he searched for the right word, ". . . *adapt* to your life. It means changing your life, almost in every way, to adapt to the bugei." As an afterthought, he added, "More is expected of a bugeisha than of an ordinary person."

He paused, sensing, I suspected, that his advice wasn't having much effect on the enthusiasm of his teenage guest. "*So 'ka*," he sighed. "We will give it a try, though, *neh*? In the meantime, I've forgotten to introduce me." He tilted his head fractionally and, with a hint of teasing, a touch of pretend grandeur, said, "I'm Kotaro Ryokichi, of the Yagyu Shinkage style of the bugei."

But I could never be so informal as to address him by his first name, or even as Mr. Kotaro. To me, he would be Kotaro *Sensei* or "revered teacher," for I was on my way to becoming a martial artist now, meaning I would have to watch such things as manners and politeness. As Sensei had warned me, more is expected of a bugeisha.

Katsujinken, satsujinken.
"The sword that gives life, not the sword that takes life,
is the goal for the Yagyu swordsman."

2.
The Sixteen Spears of Nagano

For his mischievous deeds, the god Susa-no-o-in-izumo was exiled to the land of Izumo, to a place called Torikami, near the headwaters of the River Hi. Beside the river, he lived in solitude for a time, until he saw a chopstick floating on the current. Thinking there must be other inhabitants of the land upstream, Susa-no-o set out to find them. Soon, he came upon a man, a woman, and a young maiden, all sitting at the river's bank, each of them sobbing. He gave them his name, and asked theirs in return. The man replied, "I am a god of the rural lands, called by the title of Foot-Stroking Elder. My wife is known as Hand-Stroking Elder, and our daughter is the Wondrous-Inada-Princess."

Susa-no-o then asked, "What is the reason for your tears?"

The Foot-Stroking Elder answered, "I once had eight fair daughters. But every year, the eight-forked serpent of Koshi has

9

come and devoured one. Now we are in anguish, for it is the season for the serpent to come again."

"Tell me of this beast," commanded Susa-no-o.

"It has one body, with eight heads and eight tails," said the Foot-Stroking Elder. "And its length is equal to eight valleys and eight hills. The eyes of the Koshi serpent are scarlet as winter cherries. On its back grows moss and great cypress trees, and its belly is always bloodied and inflamed."

Susa-no-o spoke then of the maiden, "If this be thy daughter, will thou offer her to me?" The Foot-Stroking Elder replied, "Humbly I would, but I know not thy august name." Susa-no-o answered, "I am the elder brother of the Heaven-Shining Deity, descended from Heaven." The Foot-Stroking Elder bowed, saying, "If that be so, with reverence would we offer our daughter to you."

To repay their kindness, Susa-no-o-in-izumo directed them in a way to destroy the serpent of Koshi. "Make a fence all around, which has eight gates within it," he said. "Atop each gate tie together platforms, and atop them place eight bowls. Into each bowl, pour some of the wine-distilled-eight-times." And so it was done, according to his bidding, and they waited until, as the Foot-Stroking Elder had truly spoken, the serpent came.

The beast entered the gates and peered into the bowls. Into each one he dipped a head and drew fully of the wine. Drunken with it, all his heads fell down, asleep. Then Susa-no-o took his ten-hand sword and cut the serpent into so many pieces that the River Hi was changed into a river of blood. He struck so mightily that his fine sword was soon broken upon a hardness within the beast's body. Thinking this strange, Susa-no-o thrust his broken sword into the flesh of the serpent, splitting it. Inside he found a perfect sword. He took the sword from the serpent's belly, and straightaway went to tell of it to the goddess Amaterasu. This is the weapon that is known as the Herb-quelling Great Sword.

The story of Susa-no-o-in-izumo and his victory over the eight-forked serpent of Koshi is recorded in Japan's oldest written source, the *Kojiki*, or *Record of Ancient Matters*, and it is evidence that, even in mythology, martial skills and the use of the sword were important qualities in Japan.

Even the islands of Japan owe their creation to a bladed weapon, according to primeval Shinto beliefs. In the ages before the earth was born, the legends say, the crepuscular nebula that was not yet the universe was inhabited by godlike *kami*. Two of the most prominent of the kami were Izanagi and Izanami who, by a decree from their divine peers, were given the task of "setting the world in order." Together they thrust a jewelled spear downward into a vast ocean below their heavenly abode and when it was retrieved, salty drops of water hardened on the spear tip. After falling from the spear, these drops grew into the chain of islands that became Japan.

More earthly residents of the land of Yamato have been using weapons of warfare, especially the sword, since the prehistoric era. Crude stone swords, unearthed in archaeological excavations there, were swung about 15,000 years ago when Japan was a primitive wilderness; the Japanese no more than wandering tribes of food gatherers and hunters.

Around the third century A.D., the civilization of the later Han Dynasty of China began to exert an influence on its island neighbors. Along with the introduction of Chinese arts and craftsmanship came Buddhism, a system of calligraphic writing, and a feudal government that achieved and maintained authority using long steel swords. Japanese makers were taught to forge these swords by Chinese smiths.

By the beginning of the Heian period (800 A.D.), Japan was stabilized into a collection of provinces further divided into wealthy estates and ruled by a strong central court in the temple-filled city of Kyoto. As a fledgling feudal kingdom, Japan had also advanced to the point where provincial leaders were growing ambitious and, consequently, nervous about the ambitions of their rivals. To insure security they gradually formed private armies of fighting men whose original title meant "house servants"—the samurai.

Probably no other warrior exemplified the qualities of the samurai, good and bad, as well as the celebrated *daimyo* and general, Takeda Shingen. Takeda ascended to his position of fame during the *Sengoku Jidai*, the "Age of Civil Strife" that wracked Japan throughout the fifteenth century, when the samurai had risen from their posts as mere martial servants to reign over the country with a rigid, military-based feudalism. Like most warriors of those days, Takeda was an adherent of Zen Buddhism and Confucian ethics. Yet more than once when his brilliant tactics were stymied, he openly resorted to treachery, as befitted the perilous way of life followed by samurai involved in a century-long civil war.

Sitting at his camp in the foothills that border Japan's broad Kanto Plain, however, Takeda reflected glumly that neither prayers nor tactics, not even subterfuge, had been of help in overcoming his present challenge. After a month of besiegement, the castle of Minowa still perched safely, maddeningly close, on a hill in front of him. Failure in this campaign was particularly frustrating to Takeda, for his specialty was in the taking of enemy fortresses: at the age of fifteen, his military career began with such a victory.

Takeda Shingen was the eldest son of Takeda Nobutora, the "Tiger of Kai Province." (As lord and military leader of his domain, Nobutora signed official papers with the last two syllables of his name, which are the Japanese characters for "tiger." That, and his typically ferocious nature, gave reason for the nickname.) While still a boy, Shingen studied the martial arts and strategy, mastering them so well that he was given his own troops to command when he was in his mid-teens. In 1534, he accompanied his father on an invasion of neighboring Shinano Province. The mission was ill-timed, occurring in midwinter, and it would have been a failure except for a daring surprise attack—carried out in deep snow and masterminded by the young Shingen—that resulted in the capture of a key enemy castle.

Any other father might have been proud of his son's accomplishments, but Takeda Nobutora was ever alert to the slightest threat to his rule, even if it came from within his own family. Sensing a germinating lust for power in Shingen, he snubbed the boy in favor of Shingen's younger brother. Once, at a meeting of his general staff, Nobutora politely served sake to his younger son, encouraging him to contribute to the conversation, ignoring Shingen entirely. The treatment rankled Shingen, who was undoubtedly even more angry because he knew his father's estimation of him was correct: his own dreams of conquest *did* rival those of Nobutora's. A few years after his first battle in Shinano, he took advantage of an opportunity to put those dreams into action and take revenge on Nobutora at the same time.

Unlike his despotic father, Shingen made it a habit to court the trust and respect of his samurai. He forged a bond of loyalty between himself and his troops that proved valuable when Nobutora left their home province of Kai to visit relatives. In his absence, Shingen persuaded his troops to stage a *coup d'etat* that was supported by Kai's civilian population, a downtrodden peasantry tired of the "Tiger's" harsh administration. When Nobutora returned, he and his company of bodyguards found themselves barred from reentering the province by the order of the new young daimyo.

The outmaneuvering of his father—with a stratagem not likely to be remembered as the most filial of devotions ever expressed by a child—was only the first step in Takeda Shingen's grand scheme to conquer the whole of central Japan and wrest control of the Imperial government from the hands of the ruling Ashikaga shogun.* The principal threat to his plan was another zealous and gifted general who credited his abilities to a belief that he was a reincarnation of Bishamonten, one of the Four Guardian Gods of esoteric Buddhism. Uyesugi Kenshin, the shaven-headed, intensely religious daimyo of Echigo Province, shared a long rivalry with Takeda that developed when Uyesugi's family and their allies were forced out of their ancestral fiefs on the Kanto, by Takeda's ever encroaching invasions.

---

*Here the reader may be confused, believing that Japan has always been under the dictate of a succession of emperors. In fact it has, but throughout much of the country's history Imperial leaders were rulers in name only. During Takeda Shingen's era, the emperor was merely a ceremonial figurehead, a living symbol of the Sun Goddess, who spent his life in courtly seclusion far removed from the provincial wars that agonized his kingdom. The actual administration of the government in Kyoto was attended to by the samurai families who were, at the time, most influential, whose leaders were the shogun, or generalissimos. In a way, the story of Japan is the story of power struggles between these incessantly warring clans, all of them vying for control of the country.

Uyesugi sought refuge in the forested hills of Echigo. He was offi-
cially adopted by the reigning daimyo there, eventually succeeding
him and building the province into a prosperous, self-sustaining
center of trade and military excellence.

Uyesugi Kenshin devoted himself to Zen Buddhism with such
fervor that he was said to lead a monk's existence, practicing
lifelong celibacy. He did not, however, neglect the temporal score
he had to settle with the young general from Kai who had so
humiliatingly deposed his family from their domain. Five times before, the forces of Takeda and Uyesugi had met, always at the same
place. On a broad valley between the Sai and Chikuma Rivers, five
battles were waged to inconclusive draws. With Takeda committing
himself to an open play for supremacy of the Kanto, Uyesugi prepared himself for the chance to deliver a fatal blow to his enemy.

To protect himself from Uyesugi, Takeda needed a block, a buf-
fer zone against the assaults he felt were sure to come from Echigo
the moment he was weakest. Situated at the edge of the Kanto ex-
panse between his Kai and Uyesugi's Echigo, the sleepy rural province of Kozuke fit the bill perfectly, for if Kozuke were held by
Takeda's army, Uyesugi could be prevented from establishing sufficient supply lines through it, making a counterinvasion of Kai impossible. Subdue Kozuke, Takeda concluded, and the threat of
Uyesugi would be nullified. In the summer of 1561, he struck there.

At the outset, the invasion of Kozuke went smoothly. Poorly
defended provincial castles were taken by quick surprise. One after
another they fell to Takeda's samurai, whose fluttering unit standards were lettered with the attributes most admired by Japan's
feudal fighting class, "Steadfast as a Mountain," "Silent as the
Wind," "Quiet as a Forest," and "Relentless as Fire."

Warfare in Japan during the long feudal age was a matter of precisely determined tactics and procedure. Armies of up to several
thousand marched into position, waiting while bowmen in close
formation loosed volleys into the enemy ranks. Following the initial engagement of archers, samurai, mounted and on foot, rushed
in wielding swords, spears, and halberds for close combat that, in

retrospect, bordered on the comically stilted.

Participants formally introduced themselves before fighting and when one samurai dispatched another he often paused to decapitate the corpse, raising the head aloft with a loudly proclaimed announcement of the deed. Personal conduct and style were far more important to the samurai than victory or defeat; this attitude led to meticulous attention being given to the accoutrements of battle. Warriors would burn incense in their helmets before going into action, so that if they were killed, their bodies would not have an unpleasant odor. Commonly displayed were distinctive *sashimono*, slender poles fastened to armor on the middle of the back, protruding a yard or more above the head. To these poles were affixed cloth banners identifying the samurai by name and rank. Armies like Takeda's even employed trained attendants to keep their armor— lacquered wooden plates connected by intricately woven silk cords—in fine polish.

Just when it seemed the soldiers of Kai would sweep through the province without a pause, their advance was tripped at Minowa, a minor castle of the Nagano family, who were loyal supporters of Takeda's enemies. At a cursory glance, Minowa didn't look like much of a threat to Takeda's progress. The smooth, sloping walls were high, but not impregnably so. Nor was its complement of defenders impressive in number: there were fewer than a thousand of them. The castle's sole defensive feature lay in its placement. Minowa was a *yamajiro,* meaning that it sat squarely on top of a high bluff, out of the reach of conventional assaults. Getting within striking range of yamajiro required an attacking force to follow a narrow road inevitably protected by a series of breastworks. Nonetheless, Takeda was confident. His bowmen scrambled into position with their seven-foot bamboo weapons, launching arrows that shattered futilely against Minowa's battlements. Cavalry and foot soldiers charged to the castle's outer fortifications, shouting their titles and past deeds as protocol demanded, as they rushed in to engage Minowa's defenders in a struggle that surged to within feet of the fortress itself before they were thrown back. Again the archers fired, followed by another charge, and the defending lines held. So it went, day after day, with Minowa remaining stubbornly invulnerable to Takeda's blitzkrieg.

Having boasted that he would smash Minowa to rubble within ten days, Takeda was soon desperate. Already a month had been wasted and sixteen thousand of his men were dead, so when spies reported that Minowa's lord, Nagano Norimasu, had died, a death which for reasons of morale the castle forces were trying to keep secret, Takeda saw an opportunity to make a change in tactics. With twenty thousand of his samurai, he charged, hoping to catch offguard the castle's new master, Norimasu's seventeen-year-old son. Beneath Minowa's white stone walls, no quarter was given. In a melee of individual clashes, Takeda and Nagano samurai fought, the cries of the wounded mingling with screamed orders and curses. Takeda concentrated his attack on the castle's rear gate and it was there that the battle grew hottest, yet each time his warriors pressed in they were repulsed by a fearful counterattack from a unit of spearmen who came whirling out of the stupefying confusion, their weapons thrusting and jabbing, to force Takeda samurai to retreat.

With the help of the seemingly possessed spearmen, the defenders appeared once more to have the advantage, but the late lord's young son, Narimori, was flushed with the excitement of the moment. In his exhilaration he raced into the torrent of blades and arrows without regard for his safety, cutting his way through the enemy with abandon until he was surrounded by them and killed.

Typical of the samurai mentality, the besieged army at Minowa were not imbued with a motivation to fight for a cause or region, but only to protect their lord's interests. At the death of Narimori they shrank back into the castle, formally surrendering a short while later.

"Bring me the captain of the spearmen who were at the rear gate," Takeda commanded. In the courtyard of Minowa he stood, his lacquered armor still dull with dust and flecked with the spittle of his horse. The tall copper crescent of the headdress on his helmet gave him a satanic countenance, a demeanor not altogether imaginary considering the orders he'd just issued upon riding into the castle keep: that all the members of the Nagano family be put to death. In an unexpected move though, considering his coldness, Takeda spared the lives of the fortress's retainers and invited them to join him in his bid for domination of the Kanto. Now his staff shifted uneasily, perspiring in their armor, and wondering how their truculent commander would deal with the leader of the "Sixteen Spears of Nagano," who had put up the fiercest resistance at Minowa.

Knots of battle-weary Takeda samurai directed their gaze in a single movement to a solitary figure who appeared, dressed in the colors of the Nagano clan. It was obvious that the fight had been hard on him, too. His corselet was chipped and dented and streaks of blood stained the blue tunic he wore over his kimono. His gait was bowed, evidence of hours spent in the saddle, so that his shin guards clicked rhythmically. Not hesitating, he approached Takeda, eyeing him levelly without a trace of the obeisance of the vanquished. He was fifty-three years old; Takeda, barely forty. The samurai's bow was long and full, as to an equal. Takeda nodded.

"I am Kamiizumi Hidetsuna, captain of the Sixteen Spears of Nagano, son of Kamiizumi Noritsuna, and a student of the Kage style of the martial arts."

The brusqueness of Kamiizumi's speech, particularly to a general of Takeda's status, revealed him instantly to be either a man who cared little for life or who was extraordinarily self-confident. Those within earshot who believed the former about the stranger held their breath. Those perceiving the latter held their smiles. Takeda, taken aback, snapped his fan shut and tapped it against his thigh to give himself a moment to think.

"You are among the most skilled warriors I've had to face, so my men tell me," he said finally, using the same frankness with which Kamiizumi had spoken. Then his words grew softer. "I regret the death of your lords, but such is karma. We who are still alive must go on, *neh*?" He paused, looking over Kamiizumi's shoulder as if he were lost in contemplation of the cryptomeria that grew in the courtyard. He spoke again, softer still. "Your value to the Nagano clan is ended. Why not join me? In such dangerous times a man could surely do worse."

The chance to serve under Takeda Shingen was tempting. His string of victories in Shinano and Kozuke were impressive, already leading to speculation in the capital that he might, in fact, succeed in his scheme for control of central Japan. Nonetheless, the leader of the Sixteen Spears declined the offer with the simple explanation that he was not really a warrior at all, only a common student of the sword who had fought at Minowa because of an obligation owed to the house of Nagano. His debt fulfilled, Kamiizumi wished nothing more than to be allowed to return to his nurturing of a new method of kenjutsu.

"My ideas for the use of the sword will have to be proven," he said to the conqueror of Minowa. "If I become your retainer and then I'm beaten or killed, I'd bring shame to you as well as to myself."

There were no ulterior motives in Kamiizumi's refusal. At a time when even rank and file samurai harbored political aspirations, his sole aim in life was to make himself a master of the bugei. To attain that goal, he had begun to suspect, meant more than the acquiring of physical technique. In the frantic chaos of battles like the one he had recently survived, Kamiizumi saw that victory depended more upon the participant's spirit and mental attitude than on his technical abilities. Over and over, he had witnessed the death of highly proficient swordsmen, killed because their concentration faltered. He had seen spearmen hesitate in their thrust and die for the split second of inaction. The way of the enlightened martial artist, he concluded, lay in a perception and perfection of the spirit to such a level that a fight might be settled before it actually started, the outcome already realized in the bugeisha's mind.

Reluctantly, Takeda allowed his former adversary to set off on his search for worthy opponents, but he refused to let Kamiizumi leave without a show of the esteem he felt for the man's martial prowess. Along with permission to leave, Kamiizumi Hidetsuna was also granted a new name by Takeda. Turning his back on the scarred walls of Minowa a few days later to devote himself to the mysteries of the bugei, he was thereafter known as Kamiizumi Nobutsuna.*

All the leaves of the autumn of 1561 had fallen, matted by October rains into a drab carpet that covered the forest with moist brown and black. In the chill dampness of the village below Minowa, charcoal makers raked their smoky fires, hoping to finish one more batch of fuel before winter set in. From further down in the valley came the distant thump-thump-thump of the cloth weaver's mallets as they beat their frames of Tamba cloth to soften the texture.

The cobblestones wet and slippery in front of him, Kamiizumi Nobutsuna of the Kage style of the bugei headed south from Kozuke, toward Kyoto.

*Another way of reading the character for "shin" is "nobu," so in effect, Takeda Shingen was bestowing part of his own name to Kamiizumi, a special honor in a society where class and a good deal of family history were determined by one's name.

3.

Matters of Concentration

"Osu!" Kotaro Sensei murmured a greeting as he strode through the door.

The mystery lady who had refused so many of my requests for instruction, and who was Kaoru, I discovered, Kotaro Sensei's wife, had a voice that intrigued. Sensei's voice, on the other hand, possessed a quality of controlled power that, more than anything else, intimidated. He spoke softly, deliberately punctuating his words.

The polo shirt and slacks he had worn at our previous meeting were gone, replaced by a quilted kimono jacket tucked into the black hakama that rustled with his step. A *bokken* was in his hand. (The wide-legged hakama are the same kind of trousers once worn by the samurai; a bokken is a sword made of hard oak, shaped and balanced like a real one. This sword is used in kenjutsu practice to avoid the injuries that would soon result from wielding a sharp steel blade.)

Following Mrs. Kotaro's instructions, I was waiting for my first lesson in what I guessed was originally the house's dining room; it had been converted into a *dojo*, a "place for learning the Way." It was expansively empty, bare except for a rack of wooden poles and bokken on one wall. On the other side, the space of a second doorway was walled up with planks and remodelled into a small alcove of the kind the Japanese call a *tokonoma*. Above the tokonoma sat a shelf with a miniature, steep-roofed house perched upon it.

Sensei paused in front of the shelf to bow slowly from the waist. He straightened, stood silently, then turned to me.

"Seiza," he said, gesturing to the floor in front of where I stood.

"Sir?"

"Seiza," he repeated briefly. "You understand? Seiza is sitting down bow."

I understood. The seiza, or formal, seated bow is done by kneeling down, first on the left knee, then on both and sitting back to rest the buttocks on one's heels. In judo and karate dojo, classes are customarily started and concluded this way.

Sensei waited for me to begin. When I did, dropping onto my left knee, I caught the smallest movement in the corner of my eye, a twitch, I thought, of Sensei's shoulders. *Wham!* The bokken smashed into my side with such force that I was pitched over, sprawling onto the floor.

"What the hell is going on?" I wondered while I stumbled to my feet. One of my elbows took the impact of the fall and I worked it back and forth gingerly, trying also to suck air back into lungs that were emptied by the force of the sword's strike. The throbbing in my side reached from hip to armpit. Sensei's command allowed no more than a couple of seconds for me to wonder what manner of sin I had committed to deserve the assault.

"Try again."

A lot more stiffly, still hurting, I tried again, getting no further than before when the bokken came at me in the same unseen way, whacking against my arm, knocking me down again. And again and again. That first afternoon as a bugeisha, I learned that pain concentrated on a specific spot can only be centralized for so long before it will become more general and so, more bearable. In fact, Kotaro Sensei wasn't really hitting me all that hard. It was the terrifying speed of the bokken and the helplessness I felt against it that made me flinch with anticipation. On the fourth or fifth try, I finally glimpsed from where Sensei's sword was coming and, jumping to the side, I succeeded in ducking out of its path. After I managed to bob out of the way when he swung at me a few more times, he nodded, indicating for me to go on. Hands at my sides, I knelt on both knees and, as I expected, Sensei struck hard with the bokken, thrusting it this time so the end of the weapon punched into my chest like a sharp fist. Once more it took repeated tries and several jolting shocks before I could twist away from the blunt point of the sword when it stabbed out at me. Sensei's gaze remained obdurate, expressionless. Still there was no explanation from him and I didn't have a chance to wonder much about it now that my senses were taking over, tuning themselves for self-preservation.

On both knees, I went ahead with the final posture of seiza, easing back to sit on my heels. Since I was facing Sensei fully and wary for the slightest movement, I figured I would be able to dodge any thrust or swing of the bokken, yet just as I pressed my bottom to my heels, my teacher reversed his grip on the sword, striking with it upward at my chin. I jerked my head aside spastically. Even though the bokken wasn't sharp, it was as dangerous as any club and with the speed and force he used, I was certain my jaw would be crushed if hit. The other blows I had begun to anticipate, but the angle of the last attack was completely unexpected. The blood in my temples pumped. Panting, every muscle strained, I waited for Sensei to bring the oak blade down. Instead, he stepped back.

"Good. Now try again."

I stood shakily to begin the whole process again. Kneeling, I pivoted away from the sword's lateral strokes. On my knees, I twisted to let the thrusts go past. Sitting back, my head cocked away in time for the upper cuts to whistle by.

"Now, not so much movement," Sensei commanded. "No need to jump a foot—" he mimed my wide, frantic dodges, "—when sword is only an inch wide." I tried to follow his advice, shifting myself as little as possible to avoid the strikes, and by the end of an hour I could often escape from the bokken without losing my balance or posture. Finally, when I made it all the way to the floor and bowed without being hit once, Sensei returned the bow and slipped into the position of seiza beside and at a right angle to me. It is customary for a Japanese of higher status to be seated at such an angle to an inferior, allowing the former to observe the latter without being watched too carefully himself. In a culture where attitudes are measured by discerning the slightest of reactions, that arrangement gives the more respected individual a considerable advantage in conversation.

Sensei sighed. "For the bugeisha," he said, "it is not enough to be alert just when holding a weapon. He must be ready for the unexpected every moment, always ready. Sitting down, getting up, eating, sleeping—all the same. The bugeisha has to be aware all the time. We call this, say in Japanese, 'zanshin'."

Along with the tremendous social and political turbulence of the Sixties there came a plague of crime. Riots erupted in most cities and with the climate of lawlessness they produced came increasing incidents of rapes and muggings and random violence. More and more Americans began looking for, if not a solution to the problems, at least a personal measure of protection from them. Many turned to the martial arts in the fanciful hope that those disciplines could mold them into invincible masters of self-defense. (Amidst their number, no doubt, were countless males partially motivated by the film exploits of the spy/playboy James Bond, who was the best-known martial artist of that era.)

In community-sponsored classes or privately run studios as well as in a variety of books published on the subject, teachers of self-protection advocated a consistently similar approach. If such and such an attack was made, they taught, such and such a response was appropriate. It was a clever assortment of joint locks, strikes, and throws that were practiced until they could be recalled at a moment's notice by the student who then went on his way, secure in the knowledge that he was safe from any threats short of a full-scale Soviet invasion.

As some of those students later discovered to their dismay, the

24

flaw in their instruction was that muggers and rapists have always had the disconcerting habit of assaulting victims in ways that might not have been covered in self-defense courses. Then too, while adroit kicks and acrobatic throws could be impressive enough in the gym where they were taught, trainees found that their tactics could be a lot more difficult to execute with an armful of groceries in tow, or while bent over, loosening the nuts on a flat tire. When I started my own martial arts training, newspaper stories appeared almost daily recounting incidents of men and women attacked while they were preoccupied with those ordinary tasks, dredging purses and pockets for car keys or waiting absentmindedly for a streetlight to change.

A principal reason why so many of those criminal assaults were successful was not because victims were unable to defend themselves physically—in many incidents they were, or would have been—but because they were unprepared mentally. Under Sensei's tutelage, I learned that the bugeisha of old faced exactly the same problem. He could be superbly skilled with a score of different weapons, but if he was caught off guard, his skills wouldn't have done him any good at all. That is why, in addition to his regular training, the bugeisha made it a constant practice to cultivate *zanshin*, literally, "continuing mind."

Zanshin can take many different forms. One afternoon, a couple of months after I had started the study of the bugei, I was upstairs at Sensei's home in the bathroom. Among the first tasks Sensei and his wife had undertaken upon moving into the house on the quiet street was to disconnect and haul out the claw-footed, cast iron tub in the second floor bathroom, to replace it with a Japanese *furo*. The wooden tub, made of slats bound together with metal bands, was compact, barely wide enough to hold two bathers. A traditional Japanese bath is filled with water heated by a fire built underneath it (a piece of sheet metal forms the tub's bottom, with a wooden rack set over it to prevent the soakers from being burned), and Mrs. Kotaro told me that her husband took considerable convincing before he decided that an open fire was not the most advisable addition to a second story bathroom in a Western home.

The toilet was on the opposite side of the room from the tub and partially screened off by a waist-high panel, but if I leaned over in the squatting, feet-on-the-floor posture nearly all Americans take when emptying their bowels, I could admire the soft, umber-stained finish of the furo's sides and wonder what it would be like to sit and soak in it. Lost in reverie, that's what I was doing when Sensei walked in unannounced to rummage for something in the bathroom closet. He ignored me, as he often did in those days when he wasn't actually teaching me. He found the towel he was looking for and left, leaving me red-faced to finish my business hurriedly.

The next day I found Sensei sitting at the living room table, drinking tea. We talked for a bit and then he pushed back his chair.

"When you use toilet, is like this?" He bent over and propped his elbows on his knees, an Oriental version of Rodin's *Thinker*.

I nodded. "Yes, Sensei."

"What would have happened yesterday," he asked, straightening up, "if I had been bad guy, come breaking in to kill you? Pants down, no way to make strong stance or defend. No zanshin. Too bad, you would have died."

Kotaro Sensei went on to show me how a bugeisha sat properly on the toilet so that even at that awkward moment he retained zanshin. I learned to pull the right leg of my pants completely off and then to sit upright, spine stretched, with my right leg folded over and that foot resting on my left thigh. In that posture he showed me how it was possible to stand quickly. Without the hobble of my pant legs flopping around my ankles, I could move freely to defend myself. Sitting straight, one leg bent in what yoga practitioners might've described as a half lotus position was also a healthy way for the body to be emptying its wastes, Sensei pointed out, allowing abdominal muscles to be strengthened and taking strain off the lower back.

"Martial arts in the toilet!" I groaned inwardly as he lectured on. When Kotaro Sensei had told me the bugei would change my life, I hadn't guessed it would include instructions for potty training, but he calmly insisted that every action of a bugeisha reflected his quality of zanshin, so I listened carefully.

Though Sensei's lesson was animated and comical—"This the way old men in Japan sit at *benjo*, squatting so not hurt bad knees. . . . Fat men bend over this way, too lazy to do right"—his intent was perfectly serious, for in the days of the samurai, bathrooms and toilets seemed to have been awfully hazardous places. At his castle in Kai Province, Takeda Shingen kept a bokken in a corner of the Japanese version of an outhouse, to insure against surprise attacks there. His precaution wasn't all that paranoid in light of the circumstances surrounding the death of Uyesugi Kenshin, his lifelong enemy. An assassin secreted himself in the open space underneath the toilet of Uyesugi's private chamber one night and while the general was sitting there the following morning he met what must have been a painful demise when he was stabbed with a short spear. To guard against similar kinds of ambushes in their baths, many samurai customarily soaked with a dirk or short sword in the steaming water beside them—a measure of security, according to annals of the time, that saved more than one life.

Actually, in the bath or anywhere else, my efforts at maintaining zanshin in those early days of my training were not spectacularly successful. An entertaining program on television, an injury at judo practice, or the passing by of a young and braless lady would instantly divert my mind from thoughts of self-defense. But I kept on practicing, imagining myself to be the modern counterpart to Matajuro, the hero of a tale told by generations of Yagyu swordsmen.

I first heard of Matajuro from Mrs. Kotaro after I absentmindedly walked through the corner of one of her iris beds and she clipped me on the back of my head with the handle of her hoe. (Between Sensei and his wife, I was beginning to take a lot of whacks with various objects around the house, and while none of them caused any real injury, the bruises they produced were difficult at times to explain to my parents and friends, who couldn't imagine what I kept bumping into.)

Matajuro was born into the Yagyu family after their clan had already gained a reputation as talented bugeisha. As a boy, his interest in the art of the blade was encouraged. He proved to be a promising but lazy pupil, in danger of never realizing the limits of his potential. In an attempt to shake him from his lethargy, his father banished him from the dojo.

Matajuro was stung by the harshness of the punishment. He was determined to dedicate himself to mastering kenjutsu—even if only to show his family how wrong they had been—so he set off to find a worthy master. The young fencer's travels took him to the province of Kii, to a region of mountains there threaded with forty-eight magnificent waterfalls, some of them cascading over four hundred feet into a rock-bordered pool where mists swirl constantly. In a thick forest at the foot of the Nachi Falls, the tallest and most beautiful of the cataracts, sits the Kumano Nachi Shrine, the site of ancient and mysterious rituals since time began in Japan.

More importantly, as far as Yagyu Matajuro was concerned, was that, according to rumors he'd heard in sake shops and inns along the highway, a sword master of incomparable skill was living near the Shrine. After a long journey, the young Yagyu reached the Kumano Shrine, where he was told by the priests to follow a barely visible path even further back into the forest. At the end, the priests said, was a senile hermit named Banzo who was reputed to have once been a swordsman. The track led Matajuro to a ramshackle hut.

"I've come to learn swordsmanship," Matajuro announced confidently, although to no one in particular since there wasn't a sign of another person about. Nervously, he softly added, "How long will it take?"

In the doorway of the hut Banzo appeared. "Ten years," he said.

"That's too long." The young Yagyu shook his head. "How about if I work extra hard and practice twice as much?"

"Twenty years," answered Banzo.

Matajuro could guess in what direction the conversation was leading, so wisely he argued no further but simply requested that he be taken as a student, to which the master readily agreed.

It was a peculiar apprenticeship. Matajuro was forbidden to handle a sword or even speak of fencing. Instead he was put to work cutting firewood, cooking for Banzo, and cleaning the hut, chores that lasted every day from before dawn until after he lit the lanterns that chased away the forest's darkness. Rarely did his master speak and never did he mention anything about teaching the boy swordsmanship.

Finally, after a year of ceaseless work, Matajuro grew frustrated, suspecting at last that he had been tricked into becoming nothing more than a servant for the surely demented Banzo. Angrily chopping at a log one day, he nearly convinced himself to find instruction somewhere else. There were plenty of teachers around who would be honored to have a member of the famous Yagyu family as a student—and plenty of conniving old swordslingers who made slaves of eager, would-be disciples, he concluded bitterly as he eyed the stack of wood still left to be cut. He sank the blade of his axe into a log, as if the cutting could remedy the problems absorbing him. He failed to notice that he was no longer alone until he was sent reeling into the woodpile by a vicious blow. (It was pleasing to me, as Sensei told me the tale of Yagyu Matajuro, to know that we had both had an initial experience in kenjutsu that included being knocked senseless.) Dazed, he looked up from the ground to find the master brandishing a length of hard green bamboo above him. Wordlessly, Banzo left as silently as he had come, leading Matajuro to conclude that his beating was for an inattentiveness to his chores.

The offspring of samurai blood was ashamed of slighting his responsibilities, even if he was plotting to leave the crazy old man. He decided to make the next chore of the day, washing Banzo's clothes, his last, but he would do such a good job of it that his master could find no fault with his work. It was a couple of hours later, while the boy was scrubbing clothes near the Falls, that Banzo struck again, harder this time, driving Matajuro splashing into the water. Behind him, Banzo roared over the crashing of the Falls.

"You expect to learn of swordsmanship, but you cannot even dodge a stick!"

Yagyu Matajuro's aristocratic pride was once more inflamed. Just as he had left his home to show his father that he could become a great fencer, he resolved to stay at the Nachi Shrine to prove the old master wrong. He began to concentrate, no matter what else he was doing, on keeping himself ready for an attack. Banzo struck five times a day, then ten, then twenty, always when his student was busy at his chores. He was so stealthy that Matajuro's only warning would be a rustle of hakama or the whoosh of the bamboo stick cutting down. Weeding in the garden, washing at the Falls, mending the hut's leaky roof, Matajuro would be occupied with one task or another, to find himself suddenly jumping at the slightest unusual noise and missing more and more of the swipes aimed at him.

When Banzo failed to connect his stick to Matajuro's head or shoulders or even to touch him with it a single time for a period of many months, he switched his strategy. In addition to the daytime assaults, he started slashing at Matajuro while the boy slept. Matajuro was forced to redouble his efforts, teaching himself to sleep lightly with his subconscious remaining alert. Grimly, he realized that the more successful he became at avoiding the bamboo stick, the more frequently it was lashed at him. Seventy, eighty, a hundred times day and night his master would appear like a ghost, swinging at him. It was growing increasingly harder for Banzo to catch him unaware, though, for his instincts were sharpened to a level almost supernatural.

On an evening four years after he had first come looking for the sword master at the Nachi Shrine, Matajuro was preparing a meal of *chirashizushi*, a steamed mixture of rice and vegetables. He was carefully peeling a burdock root for the dish when Banzo struck from behind. Matajuro didn't move from his crouching position by the fire. With one hand, he snatched up a pot lid and fended off the blow, then returned to his cooking without a pause.

That night, Banzo presented his student with a certificate of full proficiency in the art of fencing and a fine old sword. Matajuro needed neither. Without ever having taken a formal lesson or even handling a weapon, he had reached the highest peak of the bugei—the mastery of zanshin.

The walk between Sensei's house and my own home took me through a couple of acres of neatly manicured grass and trees that were preserved as a park on the homesite of the city's first resident.

Even in the heat of the September evening, when I began my training in the bugei, the park's air was pleasantly fresh. Squirrels scampered about, hiding walnuts for the coming winter. Toddlers explored with faltering steps only to be called back by parents who lounged on blankets spread under the trees, listening to the impromptu concerts of university music students. Along the border of the park ran a stream contained by WPA workers during the Depression into a channel made of natural stone and mortar. Bridges of the same construction spanned the stream.

I made it to one of the bridges before fatigue dragged me down and I slid down the face of the channel and stretched out with my back to the coolness of the bridge's concrete base. Above me hummed the tires of cars. Beyond my feet the dark ribbon of the stream trickled softly. Inside, I ached. My arms were still numbed with the battering they had taken from Sensei's bokken, and my calves and thighs throbbed from the unaccustomed exertion of crouching in seiza. In addition to the physical pain, Sensei had overwhelmed me by delivering all his instructions in a pidgin mixture of Japanese and English that continued to reel in my mind long after I had bowed a final time and left the dojo. Since his English wasn't normally that poor, I imagined that it was a plan to confuse me and cause me to quit in discouragement. Kotaro Sensei's final words to me that evening, though, were a lift.

"Next time you try make zanshin again," he said. "More practice, more practice, get better. So, hakkeyoi."

From judo, I knew "hakkeyoi" was a colloquial expression that meant "Keep at it." Alone under the bridge massaging my bruised legs until they felt good enough to carry me home, I hoped that I would.

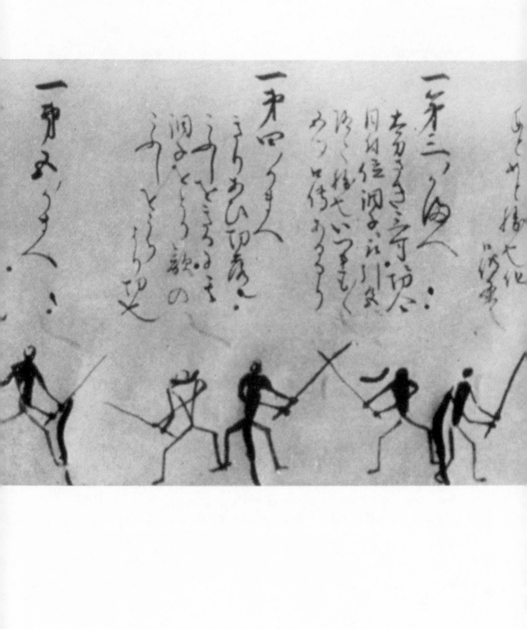

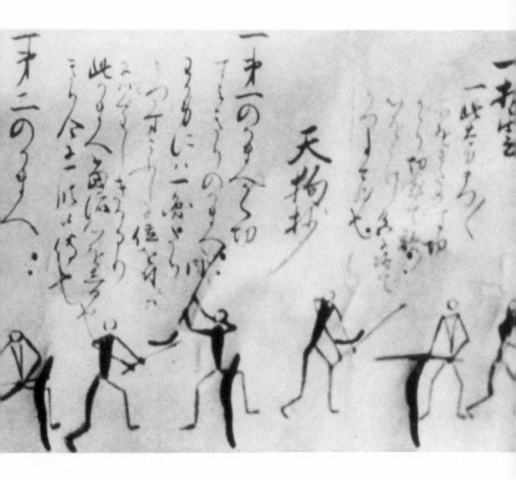

A page from the original manuscript, Heihokadensho *("A Treatise on Strategy"), by Yagyu Munenori, explaining the secrets of combat with the sword.*

4.

A Death among Peach Blossoms

In the Occident, when speaking about schools of the various arts, the word "schools" is used in a loose way. Of course, there were schools of painting, such as those that sprang up in the studios of popular artists during the Renaissance in northern Europe. And there were schools of military science like those fostered by Italy's fifteenth century *condottiere* (mercenaries), but as repositories for the comprehensive instruction of a discipline, schools in the Occident were barely adequate and usually haphazard in their methods.

Those undertaking a study of the arts of warfare in the Western world relied on inexact methods of maintaining their craft from one generation to the next. Even after the first manuals on fencing were published in England during the Elizabethan era, illustrating the basics of sabre and rapier, the most effective techniques of dueling remained the private property of the swordsmen who devised or, more likely, happened to stumble onto them in the heat of battle.

In feudal Japan, however, it was different, for there artisans of all persuasions had their *ryu*.

Like so much of the Japanese language, the full meaning of the term ryu defies an appropriate single word translation. In simplest definition, it can be used to denote a school or style of performance that's centered around any art or craft, but those words do not completely describe the place of the ryu in old and new Japan.

Perhaps the cultural tendency among the Japanese to codify and organize things led to the creation of their systematic ryu. More probably, the ryu's form of learning by depending so largely upon personal instruction was due to the lack, until recent times, of a workable printing press that could accommodate the thousands of written Japanese characters needed for publishing. Whatever the cause, from the twelfth century onward, virtually every art that was begun or practiced in Japan was characterized in its promulgation by means of individual schools or styles—the ryu.

From calligraphy to juggling to fast drawing a sword, few skills were so minor in scope that they lacked the academic guidance of the ryu. During the country's long medieval age, for instance, three major schools of *kado*, or the techniques of flower arrangement, were established, each with several variations. The Noh theater encouraged the formation of ryu that taught acting. Students of the Ogasawara ryu were devoted to the task of learning the intricacies of formal etiquette. While many of these schools have become extinct with the passing of the centuries, representative ryu of most of the arts of Japan still flourish in very much the same way today as they did when they were founded five or six hundred years ago.

That the ryu have been able to retain their teachings and traditions over so many years is attributable to the unique way in which adherents to a ryu were selected and educated in its particular art. In an arrangement similar to the master-apprentice institution that evolved in preindustrial Europe, a sensei, having been trained in the same fashion himself, would gather about him a group of students who lived and learned under his invariably stern tutelage.

The disciples, in turn, supported the sensei financially and if his school was big enough, taught newcomers who did not yet rate the attention of the master.

Life as a pupil of the ryu was not easy, whether its curriculum was swordsmanship or pottery. Often the new trainee went through a lengthy period of personality testing where his only duties were menial housekeeping chores, cutting wood, or attending to the personal needs of the sensei and his family. One famous swordsmith of the fourteenth century refused to let his charges attempt any work near his forge at all for five years, except for tending the bellows. A master storyteller refused to teach his performing secrets to students until they had repeated the same simple tale over and over to such an extent that it was memorized in every detail without flaw.

The harshness of the ryu's discipline accomplished two ends. First, it weeded out all of those aspirants not sincerely interested in the art. Since the sensei had only a limited amount of time to spend in instruction, he couldn't afford to waste it on a student who was anything less than completely dedicated to eventual mastery. Second, the protracted internship at the lowest rungs of the ryu ladder gave the student a chance to observe the fundamentals of his craft so frequently that they became ingrained in him. The disciple squatting day after day, month after month at the bellows of the swordmaker had little else to do but watch his master at the initial stages of hammering out one of the fine steel blades of the samurai and by the time he was allowed to begin learning the trade in earnest, it was a totally familiar operation.

In these ways, the ryu system differed little from the European custom of apprenticeship. The Japanese ryu were distinctive, however, in that an imparting of the mechanics of the craft, the *shoden* and *chuden* ("first and second stages of teachings"), were considered to be only a partial aspect of a student's education. What really mattered was the sensei's careful transmission of the metaphysical principles of his ryu to his most promising disciples. In folktales of old Japan, these secret teachings, known as *hoben* ("special skills"), *okuden*, or *okugi* ("hidden methods"), figure prominently, bestowing superhuman abilities upon the possessor.

35

In truth, the secrets were usually less fantastic. The okuden of a flower arranging school might consist simply of some techniques that would keep flowers fresh once they were placed in a container. Closely guarded secrets passed on by swordsmiths late at night in their workshops were often merely practical advice on how to temper a blade.

Other, more mystical okuden—believed by practitioners to be the essence of their ryu—consisted of ritual incantations or designs, the use of which led to success in mastering the art. A potter would divulge to his favorite pupil the words of a prayer to be chanted when firing his kiln, knowing that, in turn, the student would pass on the secret. In this emphasis on the hidden and spiritual facets of the arts the ryu became much more than a school. Disciples were almost like the children of their sensei and the traditions and customs of the ryu assumed the importance of sacred possessions to be handed down with great care and ceremony, generation after generation.

Not surprisingly, it was during the Sengoku Jidai, the "Age of Civil Strife," that the ryu of the bugei developed to their fullest extent. Throughout most of the twelfth century, the mighty clan of the Hojo family had managed to enforce a stability resembling peace, preventing the country's daimyo from escalating their continual disputes over land into open war. Two times, once in 1274 and again in 1281, Hojo samurai had held off the first attempts at an invasion of Japan when the Kublai Khan's hordes swept into Kyushu's Hakata Bay. With the unexpected aid of the *kamikaze*, the "divine winds" of a typhoon, the Hojo clans prevented the Mongols from gaining even a foothold in Japan and left most of the Khan's proud fleet at the bottom of the bay. However, during the siege, frictions and feuds arose and before long, the authority of Hojo rule was threatened by a score or more scheming daimyo.

By 1333, the Hojo regent Yoritomo, along with his family and nearly 800 loyal samurai, was driven from his court in Kamakura. They fled to the temporary safety of the hills surrounding the city, taking refuge in caverns. As the enemy closed in, his family, then his warriors, and finally Yoritomo himself all took what was fast becoming the accepted course for a samurai seeking to avoid capture or humiliation. Drinking a farewell cup of sake together, the Hojo clan knelt, one by one in the cavern's flickering torchlight and drove swords into their bellies.

The fall of the Hojo government gave way to chaos in Japan. They were succeeded by the Ashikaga family, who held the position of shogun for two centuries. Their control, though long-lived, was never anywhere near absolute, and long festering rivalries between daimyo gave way to more serious discord and a nation-wide civil war that was to last over a hundred years.

Nearly every province in Japan knew the horrible destruction wrought by major battles and the harrowing disruption of normal life brought about by the ceaseless warfare of the Sengoku Jidai. Daimyo directed armies of samurai retainers from the castles in their home fiefs, sending them out to fight and die in compliance with the unforgiving principles of their *bushido*. It was an age when the crafts of battle became polished and refined from frequent use, so naturally, with so much opportunity for practice, the samurai began to take an interest in improving his trade. He sought out the instruction of the most qualified of his peers who soon found themselves in the full-time occupation of teaching the methods of killing with the weapons of the day: the sword, spear, halberd, and bow. These teachers were the founders of the bugei ryu.

According to Yamada Jirokichi, a master swordsman of the middle 1800s and author of the *Kendo Ron* (Treatise on the Way of the Sword), there were originally three major ryu of swordsmanship. The oldest of them was called the Shinto ryu, founded by a fifteenth century warrior named Iizasa Choisai Ienao whose style, as its title indicated, was closely connected with the traditions and theology of Japan's oldest religion. The second important ryu was the Itto style. *Itto* means "one sword," an appropriate name, for students of the Itto school had a deserved reputation for the single stroke quickness of their swords.

About the third school little was known among martial exponents of the time. It was called the Kage, or "Shadow" style, an appellation that gave few clues to its sources and even fewer to the particulars of its techniques. Students and masters of the school seemed unwilling to discuss it at all with fencers of other ryu. They remained silent in response to the rumors begun by the common folk that Kage ryu strategy had been given to swordsmen ascetics who trained secretly under the guidance of wild mountain goblins and spirits.

In 1563, two years after he and his spearmen had been defeated at the Minowa Castle, the man who knew most about the Kage style of swordsmanship stood watching a cockfight in the yard of a *shokubo* inn that was run by priests catering to the needs of Buddhist pilgrims and other travelers passing through the Shiga highlands.

One russet and black, the other white, the Cochin cocks were eager to spring from their positions on opposite sides of a big woven bamboo basket, their thick leg muscles coiled, hackles bristling. The sandal maker who had come from his shop down the street to join the crowd of onlookers assured Nobutsuna that the white cock was a clear favorite to win, but a pair of palanquin bearers, relieved from their duties for the time being and grateful for the diversion, were betting a palmful of hard earned silver ryo on the russet. Their excited chattering was lost in the shouts of encouragement accompanying the birds as they were released to burst into the air, clashing when they fell in a flurry of kicking spurs.

Besides the sandal maker, the palanquin bearers, and Nobutsuna, the noisy cluster of spectators included a cross section of Japanese village life. An amused doctor, dignified in his dark silk kimono, stood next to the more plainly dressed proprietor of a sake shop. Crouched on the bare ground before them was a cooper, sinewy and naked except for his wrapped loincloth. Four of the shaven-headed priests who maintained the inn looked on, laughing at a shared witticism, and another squatted close to the scene of the combat, chin in hand, seeing in the birds' struggle, perhaps, a vivid Buddhist allegory.

Kamiizumi Nobutsuna took note of all of them. For a samurai of his experience, it was almost an instinctive habit to survey faces in a crowd, alert for the first sign of danger. Judging by their sturdy clothes, Nobutsuna saw that there were also a few travelers like himself among the group, most of them, he assumed, guests at the inn, and almost all of them absorbed by the miniature battle being waged in the bamboo basket.

All except one. The man was obviously not a local inhabitant. His hakama was gathered up at the legs for easier walking, his sandals were of a heavy duty construction, and a quilted *haori* vest worn over his kimono protected against the still chilly winds that blew off the slopes of nearby Mt. Asama. He was at the front of the animated crowd, yet like Nobutsuna, his attention was only partially directed at the cockfight. His glances swivelled about, taking in every face. When his gaze met Nobutsuna's neither averted. Between them, the cocks fought on, beaks open in clucking gasps, but their duel was of no importance compared to the still indiscernible one commencing above them in the focused, unyielding eyes of Nobutsuna and the traveler.

"Hikiwake!" cried the white cock's handler. He plunged a hand through the basket opening to grasp his animal's legs and separate the fighters. The russet cock's owner agreed reluctantly to the call of a draw since neither bird seemed able to go on and their feathers, tinged with blood, littered the ground. The throng of spectators slowly dissolved into smaller groups already beginning arguments that would continue at the sake shop, arguments over which cock had displayed more fighting spirit.

Nobutsuna and the traveler remained rooted for a moment, alone together over the empty, feather strewn basket. Finally, the man nodded briefly, turned and walked away. Nobutsuna understood the gesture perfectly. Though neither had even touched the swords they both wore, the duel had begun. Unlike the cockfight, Nobutsuna reflected, almost with amusement, there could be little expectation of a draw. He returned to the inn, to eat supper and to wait.

Aside from a prestigious new surname, Kamiizumi Nobutsuna didn't have much going for him when he left the castle at Minowa and began his pilgrimage in search of perfection with the sword. In fact, the chances for his very survival were something short of slight. During the fifteenth century the countryside of Japan was sprinkled with samurai and bugeisha,* all off on similar journeys, searching for some ultimate secret of martial arts prowess, or, more often, bent on proving the skills they had already gained. Challenges for duels were commonplace. Wandering warriors embarked on *dojo arashi*, "dojo storming," where they visited every school or fencing master they could find to request a match. Occasionally these duels ended when one martial adept displayed an obvious superiority, forcing an opponent to admit defeat, but usually their outcome was decided by death. Simply put, had the life insurance business existed in those days, the bugeisha would certainly have fit into the high risk category, for they never knew when or where a rival might try to cut them down.

The message Nobutsuna waited for came later in the evening, delivered by a servant at the inn while Nobutsuna sat in his room drinking tea with the two Kage ryu disciples who were accompanying him in his travels, Jingo Muneharu and Hikida Bungoro.

Hikida, Nobutsuna's nephew as well as his student, read the note aloud. "Nobutsuna Esquire, I humbly request a lesson from you in the art of fencing. If it will be acceptable, I shall be awaiting you at the crossroads near the Etsu stream at dawn tomorrow." The note was signed with the name Nagayuki Kenzo, of the Kashima ryu.

The window shutters of the room on the inn's second floor had been opened, admitting the evening's cool air and allowing Nobutsuna the view of the surrounding hills, tinged with spring's green. He seemed absorbed in the vista. Jingo shifted his weight and tugged at the corner of his floor cushion. Hikida, still holding the note,

---

*The titles *samurai* and *bugeisha* are not necessarily synonymous. Technically, the samurai (more properly known during their own time as *bushi*) were a class of professional soldiers that comprised the private armies of the feudal daimyo. "Bugeisha" refers to any individual who undertakes a practice of the bugei, the military (*bu*) crafts (*gei*) of Japan. While it is true that, during most of that country's history, classes other than the bushi's were either prevented by law or opportunity from engaging in the martial arts, there were many well-known bugeisha who, for one reason or another, were able to achieve a high level of proficiency in the arts even though they were not members of the military clique. This became more common in the sixteenth and seventeenth centuries.

finally cleared his throat to gain Nobutsuna's attention. With a measured calm that had grown perceptibly in the long pause after he had heard the message, the swordsman spoke to Jingo.

"Kashima fencers take pride in the speed of their footwork," he said slowly. "Watch this Nagayuki fellow closely tomorrow and you may learn something about striking as the lead foot advances."

Jingo's upper body inclined in a bow, but he did not ask any questions. His master's ways he knew well. The politely worded invitation to kill or die had been delivered and received. From that moment until the completion of the duel's final blow, Nobutsuna's concentration would be narrowed to an almost superhuman degree that left little room for any other thought. With him, Jingo and Hikida continued in silence to watch the shadows lengthen on Mt. Asama.

The foothills of the Shiga highlands are steep and furrowed and even into late spring, funnels of snow stay frozen white near their summits. Asama towers over every other peak in the vicinity, wearing an especially heavy coat of snow even though at its base, the orchards of the peach farmers have burst into acres of pink blossoms.

A local farmer was out in the orchards early the next morning, making an inspection of the trees that floated in waves of a fog that pooled in the valleys each night. Their dainty pinkish blossoms scattered on the ground around him as he ambled through the rows, like the perfect fingernails, he reflected, of a girl he had met in Kyoto. The morning's clammy mists would burn away soon, revealing the mountain heights in all their splendor and by then he would be with the others, thinning the spongy tiers of barley seedlings on the mountain's lower slopes. The lone farmer didn't have any particular need to be in the orchard. The peaches had been growing there with a minimum of care since his grandfather's day and it wouldn't be necessary to prop up their branches, heavily laden with green fruit, for several months. It was an affection for the verdancy of the season and for the solitude of the orchard that drew him there; for in Japan, with its tiny houses and crowded families, the chance to be completely alone, to think an uninterrupted thought or scratch contentedly any place that itched, was a singular occasion.

He saw no one amid the fog-blurred ranks of pink. That he was, in fact, not alone came entirely as a feeling at first, a sensation of the presence of another that grew stronger as he ambled farther down the misty rows, getting closer to the highway that led back toward the village. He didn't actually see the swordsman until he was only two rows away. Even in the fog the farmer was close enough to recognize the man as an outsider to the village. The swordsman squatted with one knee pressed to the ground, absorbed with the task of tying back his kimono sleeves with a silk cord, leaving his forearms bare. Twisted into the bindings of his hakama was a darkly lacquered scabbard with the hilt of a three-foot sword extending out at the level of his waist. At the sight of the sheathed sword, the farmer involuntarily drew back his step and his breath, his eyes bulging with sudden alertness. For the slightest infraction of propriety, even imagined, a commoner like himself could be hacked to pieces by a swordsman of samurai rank who enjoyed perfect immunity from any legal retribution for the act.

He watched with his whole being to determine if his presence had been noted. If he crabbed backward, he thought frantically, he might be able to scoot away without being discovered. Of course, it was possible the sword-carrying stranger meant him no harm. He could have been a penniless traveler unable to afford a night at the inn, spending it instead under the protection of the peach trees. But he was well-dressed and his clothes weren't damp with the morning's dew. The farmer tried to shrink himself into a huddled ball. One could not be too careful.

"Nobutsuna sama! I am here."

The farmer jerked when the voice cut into the milky morning air with a knifing impatience. His efforts at staying concealed in the rapidly disappearing mists prevented him from noticing the arrival from the village road of a second man, also a stranger and also armed. If his startled little jump caught the attention of the swordsman near him, no sign was given. The still figure beneath the tree straightened and brushed at the knee of his hakama, then separated himself from the border of the orchard to stand near the middle of the road.

"I am Nagayuki Kenzo, Nobutsuna sama." Again the newcomer used the politest form of address, showing his awareness of Nobutsuna's reputation as a warrior. He bowed and narrowed the distance between them. Nobutsuna returned the bow, holding his head out at an angle so that his neck was not exposed, a courtesy of samurai etiquette.

"I am Kamiizumi Nobutsuna, of the Kage ryu."

There was little difference in their overall appearances. Like Nobutsuna, Nagayuki wore a split hakama and the sleeves of his bright blue kimono were also bound up with string. He had on the same haori overvest he had worn the day before. Wrapped around his waist was a wide cotton *obi* into which were thrust two swords, one long, the same size as Nobutsuna's, the other shorter by a foot and a half. To indicate that he intended no surprise Nagayuki stretched his left arm down slowly until his fingertips touched the side of the scabbard of his long sword.

"Shall we begin?"

Nobutsuna raised his hand. "Two of my students are to be here to watch and learn. Could we wait a bit?"

To a samurai of Nagayuki's modest rank, the opportunity for recognition and advancement was rare. Since the death of his lord a year before, he had become a *ronin,* a "man of the waves." Some ronin starved, knowing no other occupation by which to make a living, and many others turned to banditry. Nagayuki was grateful for the occasional employment he had found as a bodyguard to wealthy merchants. The pay was sufficient and if he could keep himself from getting killed it wouldn't be long before he would find another lord in need of his services. If he carried with him the reputation of a man who had defeated a samurai of Nobutsuna's stature, his services would be considered all the more valuable.

For two weeks Nagayuki had known that he and the great swordsman were in the same area. Three days earlier he had been told of Nobutsuna's exact location at the inn. Suddenly the sleepless nights, the vacant hours of wondering and speculating, the tasteless meals forced down only to come up again almost immediately, all of the wrenching anticipation of the encounter began. The morass of bubbling fears his insides had become would have reduced a lesser human being to a state of quivering paranoia, but Nagayuki Kenzo was a samurai by birth and upbringing and while he may have been ambitious, by no standards could he have been judged a coward.

Now, however, he sensed his carefully cemented composure crackle ever so slightly. His attention was so intensely focused on the moment, expecting it to play itself out to an imminent conclusion, that Nobutsuna's unforeseen delay threatened to slip the delicately balanced gears of his timing, preventing them from catching again until it was too late. He struggled for self-control, while searching for a distraction.

"Only two students are coming?"

Nobutsuna answered affirmatively.

"Who then is watching us from over there in the orchard?"

Nobutsuna's expression hinted at something close to a smile. "A peasant," he said matter-of-factly, shifting his weight to his right, opposite the side of his body where his sword was slung. "He came stumbling up through the rows while I was waiting, making enough noise for a troop of monkeys. . . . Harmless."

Nagayuki crossed his arms and shrugged. Peasants, as both he and Nobutsuna knew, were like toothpicks: not especially attractive to behold or worthy of any comment, they were, nevertheless, necessary for fulfilling a lowly task. He turned inward, concentrating on calming himself with a rhythmic series of breathing exercises taught to exponents of the Kashima school.

The ensuing silence was embarrassingly awkward. Men bent on killing one another have a certain reticence toward conversation at the time.

Shortly, Hikida and Jingo hurried up, breathless. As one, they bowed to their master and nodded respectfully to the man who would try to take his life. Hikida murmured the reason for their tardiness. On leaving the village they had missed a directional sign in the fog. After his explanation, both retreated out of the way, positioning themselves at the edge of the ditch. Behind them in the orchard, the farmer wondered and watched as if he were witnessing a spectacle from a foreign world.

Nagayuki drew his sword first. It came free from the scabbard with a leathery sound, although the scabbard was actually made of soft wood. He grasped it with both hands and settled himself into a stance of such solidity that he appeared to be rooted to the earth. Nobutsuna slid his weapon out and held it vertically, the razor tip pointing straight up. Balanced on the balls of his feet he came half a stride closer to Nagayuki. In contrast to his opponent's posture, he gave the impression of having become as light as a dry winter leaf, an illusion heightened, from the three onlookers' points of view, by the fingers of mist curling around him.

Deai is the word used to describe the inception of movement in an attack. It is the final linkup from the brain's authoritative impulses to the compliance of muscle and bone—stillness erupting into action. Nagayuki's deai was electrifying. One instant he was at rest, the next he had plunged into the gap between himself and Nobutsuna, already completing the initial movement Nobutsuna had warned Jingo to watch for, but it was much too quick to be perceived intellectually. As he attacked, Nagayuki pulled his sword above his head, bringing it into position for the stroke downward and adding to the impetus of his charge. In relationship to his rival's stunning speed, Nobutsuna seemed hardly to move at all. His bent legs glided forward slowly together, almost lazily, when he suddenly raised his sword, still vertical, high above him.

The farmer's first thought was that Nobutsuna had somehow struck something in the air, glancing away his half-completed blow. That he was wrong was apparent and immediately horrifying to him.

Nagayuki was dying before he slumped onto the road, carried along by the force of his attack, yet drained of its life-affirming power. From his forehead to the base of his nose a gash leaked blood that soaked the damp soil, turning it an even richer shade of brown. The duel that began when his eyes met Nobutsuna's over the thrashing gamecocks was over. The lesson was concluded.

Twenty minutes passed before the farmer lifted his arm to

wipe away the grimy film of dried perspiration that caked his face and it was nearly an hour before he trusted himself to stand, loosening a shower of peach blossom petals from his shoulders. He crept away from the orchard road and the solitary corpse without looking back.

5.

Autumn and Other Things Japanese

On a nameless sand spit in the swift straits of Kanmon, which separates Kyushu from Honshu, Miyamoto Musashi, Japan's most famous samurai folk hero, won the duel that was to secure him a place of honor in stories, romantic novels, and eventually on the movie screen. Musashi's opponent in the match was Sasaki Kojiro, whose phenomenal talent in swordsmanship was accentuated by the distinctive weapon he used, a blade nearly two feet longer than those carried by most swordsmen of the era. Given the reach of his sword and his fearsome reputation—according to one legend he proved his expertise to fellow passengers on a ferry crossing of Lake Biwa by shearing the topknot off a samurai who had gotten into an argument with him, drawing and cutting before the samurai had time to duck—the odds were stacked heavily against Musashi, who, at that time, was still relatively unknown, a shabbily dressed country bumpkin from Mimasaka Province.

Not only did Musashi kill Sasaki, however, he did it with a wooden sword he carved from a spare oar while being rowed out to the site of the duel. Musashi knew, as did many other of Japan's best swordfighters, that the bokken, far from being a supplemental training aid in kenjutsu, was every bit as lethal as a sharp steel blade.

The bokken in my hands was a curved piece of oak, three feet long and polished to a warm smoothness. Kotaro Sensei was drilling me in the simplest movement of the Yagyu ryu's curriculum: raising the sword above my head and bringing it down along the same path in an uninterrupted motion. He had to stop and correct me constantly. At first I held the bokken the same way one would grip a baseball bat or a golf club, with my hands as close together as possible. Sensei showed me that by separating them, right hand on top near where the guard would be on a *katana*, or real sword, and my left hand almost on the knob at the end of the hilt, I could move my wrists more freely and give the sword a wider range of play. Then he transformed my jerky chopping into a more natural swing, all the while adjusting the parts of my body that refused to cooperate.

"Feet turned so. Legs bent for springing to take shock like shock absorbers for car. Elbows same way. Both feet slide same time forward. Sword up"—not up, but exactly parallel to the floor—"cut now, cut, cut, cut."

Even though I was only slashing at the air in front of me, if my knees and elbows didn't remain flexible my body would wrench against the force of the bokken as it came down. As it was, my wrists were already aching with the unaccustomed weight of the weapon and instead of looking as if I was tugging on a bell rope like Sensei wanted, my cuts resembled those of an arthritic and inebriated woodchopper.

The details—as well as the repetition required to learn them—were endless. Kotaro Sensei's warning to me that more was expected from a bugeisha caused me to think he meant I would be forced to endure the tedium of training and to devote myself to the study of the sword or spear or whatever. As my education in the bujutsu progressed, I found that the expectations were far wider. In a variety of subtle ways, I began to conform to a Japanese manner of doing certain things; this manner was further refined by Kotaro Sensei and his wife into the samurai way of doing them. They were the sort of lessons that turned a quiet evening meal into an obstacle course of mental alertness and manual dexterity.

I learned how to eat with *hashi* (chopsticks) at the Kotaros table, chasing wriggly pieces of vegetables across plates and picking rice grains from my bowl. When I had achieved a presentable level of skill with hashi, I was instructed in how a bugeisha must use them. Normally, hashi are pushed straight into the mouth along with the piece of food held between them. After a couple of times of observing me eat in that fashion, Sensei casually reached over and popped the chopsticks on the ends with his palm, jamming them against the back of my throat like the tongue depressor of a maniac physician. Not looking forward to another impromptu tonsillectomy, I straightaway mastered the knack of turning the sticks sideways as they approached my mouth—not as a precaution against a dinnertime assailant, but to conduct myself with a samurai bearing.

The rice bowl became the object of the next lesson. A Japanese with normal eating habits grasps his bowl on its underside with his fingertips and lifts it to the level of his mouth. When I did it that way, Sensei calmly tipped the bowl into my face. Then he showed me how to hook my thumb and forefinger over the bowl's rim, just as samurai in Japan had done centuries before to eliminate the danger of being attacked while eating.

Ordinarily, martial artists don't have to spend a lot of time studying knots. The belt worn in judo or karate is wrapped twice around the waist and tied in a simple square knot. For the bugeisha, though, knotcraft was one more art to be practiced and my expertise at it was soon elevated to that of an Eagle Scout's. Instead of the narrow sash of judo or karate, my jacket was kept closed by a wide band of cloth like a kimono's obi that was twisted around my middle several times and then fastened in a complicated "figure ten" knot. (The name comes from the Japanese character for ten, which resembles a cross or a "plus" sign.) Over the obi I wore a hakama like Sensei's, with four cords of differing lengths that had to be knotted and wrapped in exactly the right way to prevent the skirt from loosening and falling down during practice. There were specific knots used for tying shut the bag where swords are stored, knots for attaching the silk cord *sageo* to a sword's scabbard, and knots for fastening the sageo to the obi once the scabbard is placed there.

Not all the details heaped upon me during those first few months with Sensei were so technical. Some involved the etiquette of the dojo, manners and courtesies that had little application in the twentieth century but were a function of the bushi's society and therefore important to the continuance of his martial arts. Still, for a boy raised with the informality of jeans and junk food, the rigid conventions of feudal Japan were often hard to fathom.

Besides his left and right foot, for instance, a bugeisha in the dojo must also bear in mind that he has a *shimo ashi* and a *kami ashi*. The foot nearest the left side of the dojo is the shimo ashi; the one on the right side, the kami ashi. (*Kami* means "upper." The little house I saw on the wall of the dojo before my first lesson was the home of the spirits of Sensei's ancestors and so was called the *kamiza*, or "seat of the upper deities.") In entering or leaving the dojo or approaching the kamiza, I had to be careful about having the correct foot in the correct place. After being reprimanded for forgetting to keep my steps in proper order, I once suggested to Sensei that he put down the footprints like those on dance studio floors. The flippancy failed to make the transition between our cultures. Perhaps, for my sake, it was just as well.

After Sensei's bokken had taught me the folly of bowing without remaining alert, I went on to learn Oriental etiquette in its diverse forms. From a fractional lowering of the eyes with a nod to a forehead on the floor prostration, the wide range of bowing methods was a way of establishing rank or social position for the bushi and everyone else in Japan. One family, the Ogasawara, became the Emily Posts of the fifteenth century, codifying and providing instructions for bowing in a huge volume of etiquette procedures. Every movement of the bows was intended to convey meaning and every meaning was full of subtlety.

Not all the details of an education in the bugei were as minor as leaving the dojo with the appropriate foot or inclining my head at the right angle when bowing. Language was very important, for Kotaro Sensei and his wife spoke little English at home. Even when spoken slowly and with deliberate emphasis, the simplest of words in Japanese can be terribly difficult to understand, and, unlike many European tongues that share a common ancestry in Latin, there are no dependable clues available for translating meaning. To hear a conversation between husband and wife carried on with rapid-fire staccato and imperious brusqueness and be unable to detect even the general intent of the exchange was stunning and frustrating—and frequently led me to the wrong conclusions.

"Uchi no hito!" Mrs. Kotaro would snap briskly from upstairs.

Sensei, puttering in the kitchen, would fire back, "Nan dai?"

"Ima nanji des'ka?"

"Sanji-han!"

"So'ka."

Alone in the dojo, I would be rolling my eyes in acute embarrassment at overhearing what I took to be the opening volleys of a wicked fight, but what sounded to me to be the onset of a bickering quarrel was only Mrs. Kotaro asking the time and Sensei telling her it was half past three. And it could be worse. Listening to them making up a shopping list was enough to make one want to suggest a marriage counselor.

Some of the details of my education in the bugei were equally prosaic, though they were perhaps even more important to my growing up than training itself. Little, for instance, prepared me for life around a middle-aged Japanese woman. And even had there been, Kaoru Kotaro was not always the typical woman of her generation.

Kaoru's great grandfather, Masao Yoshioka, had been one of Kyoto's most renowned painters and calligraphers, a direct descendant of a warrior clan and a samurai himself. His marriage to a daughter of a prosperous Kyoto sake merchant secured the financial position of the Yoshioka family, and so Kaoru was born and raised in wealth. As a young girl, she took for granted everything from her spacious home in Kyoto's garden district to her elegant silk *furisode* kimono. Her days were filled with the preoccupations of the offspring of Kyoto's privileged; lessons in flower arranging and in learning to pluck with a polished bone plectrum, the long twanging cords of that most Japanese of musical instruments, the *koto*. She was carefully shielded from the harsher realities of the world outside Kyoto, shielded from the atrocities her countrymen committed against China in the twenties and thirties and shielded from all the other events that brought Japan into a world war in the forties.

Kyoto was spared virtually all of the terrible bombing that ravaged most of the rest of Japan during that war, and so through Bataan and Guadalcanal and the Battle of Okinawa, life continued on with some measure of normalcy for Kaoru. But while Kyoto survived, the Yoshioka's sake-brewing facilities in Osaka were reduced, along with the rest of that port city, to a burned-out skeleton. For her family, the Occupation and the emergence of a new Japan meant a desolate period of privation and near bankruptcy until they could reestablish their business. Kaoru remembered that time for me one afternoon, recounting the day the antiques buyer from down the street came to visit the Yoshioka home.

"That first time, he didn't take so much, just some lacquerware. But then he came back, and then again, maybe twice a month, and he left with more and more." Her eyes softened in recollection of furniture, and kimono, and finally her great-grandfather's paintings, all carried away to raise money to pay growing debts.

"Mother and Father sold much of what they owned," she told me, "but never the belongings of their children. So even though I was old enough to understand what was happening, and I should have, I was very selfish. I tried just not to think about it." Then one day Kaoru's older brother brought her face-to-face with the desperation of their situation. After demanding a promise of secrecy from her, he told her that he was going to sell the Cherry Tree Sword to the antiques buyer to contribute to the family's meager finances.

The Yoshika's Cherry Tree Sword was a family secret and a private joke among them. It was a beautiful weapon, six generations old, and had been given to Kaoru's brother on his fifth birthday.

After the war's end, rumors began circulating that the American authorities would soon be around to confiscate weapons in private homes, to insure the safety of the Occupation Forces. Like other fine swords all over Japan, the Yoshioka blade was wrapped in cloth, sealed in a wooden box, and hidden in the hollow of an old cherry tree in the back yard. It was from there that her brother retrieved it, while Kaoru stood lookout for parents who they both knew would never have allowed so important an heirloom to have been sold. She went with him to hand the sword over to the dealer, who paid for it a price slightly less than what amounted to fifty cents for every year of the weapon's age

"Then I knew what losing the war was all about," she told me simply. Two days later, she made her own trip to the dealer, carrying her most precious possession, a Yuzen kimono, its delicate pattern of maple leaves dyed in the Ebanui process.

The privations and hardships of the Occupation left their mark on Kaoru. While she never lost the gentility of her upbringing, deep inside she was somehow tempered by the experiences of the postwar poverty, I think, resulting in a woman who was an enigma to me. Often Japanese women of Kaoru's age tend to be gregarious, gathering at one another's houses for the flimsiest of reasons to talk. Kaoru, though, kept to herself; other than her husband, she had few people who could have been called friends. She had learned to live within herself, it seemed, to endure and to experience life's pleasures and pains, never showing any more feeling about either of them than she wanted to. On occasion, we would go for hikes along an Ozark stream bed together and there she would explain to me, with the most perceptive sensitivity, why this rock had qualities of shape and hue that would add to the beauty of a Japanese-style garden, and that one did not. Yet I approached subjects like loneliness or love with trepidation, for she was rarely willing to talk about them. As she told me once, "It isn't that we are without feelings, it is only that we prefer to cultivate them in private."

Mrs. Kotaro went on cultivating her feelings in a private, hidden way, with the same care in which she cultivated her iris in the yard. Even though she would never be openly affectionate toward

53

me in public, she gradually developed a kind of signal aimed at me when she was proud of me or happy with what I'd done. Looking at me without a word, she would slowly close both eyes, then open them, with the faintest trace of a smile on her face. It was barely noticeable, and always silent, but in her own way, I came to know that Kaoru was speaking volumes to me.

Mrs. Kotaro was forced to speak volumes to me in another area of our relationship, though, when she undertook the task of teaching me to speak Japanese.

As hard as Sensei pushed me in training with the bokken, his wife was even more relentless in teaching me *Nihongo*— Japanese—once I expressed an interest. Her method was to sit across from me at the dining room table and pronounce a word, getting me to repeat it exactly. I mean *exactly*.

"Sake," she said with labored emphasis.

"Sake," I replied for the fifth time.

"No, no. Sa*ke* is word for alcohol drink. Word for salmon fish is *sa*ke. Try to say sake, make 'ke' part come out lower, like you are sad."

"Sake. *Sa*ke. Sake," I repeated, though my "ke" was never once mournful enough to please her.

Strangely, while Mrs. Kotaro demanded that my Japanese be painfully correct, she rarely made any attempt to improve her marginal English and, in fact, became miffed at the mildest hint that her accent was irregular. We were at a MacDonald's restaurant one evening and it was her turn to place her order with the girl at the counter.

"May I help you?" the girl bubbled.

"Please," replied Mrs. Kotaro. "Duburo hamabuguru an' a miriku shaku."

"I beg your pardon. Could you repeat that?" She looked at Mrs. Kotaro as if reading her lips would be an aid. Irritated at MacDonald's practice of hiring workers who didn't understand perfectly good English, Mrs. Kotaro repeated the order with the same results. I interrupted.

"She'll have a double hamburger and a milk shake."

"Oh . . . . What flavor is that shake?"

Without the slightest hesitation Mrs. Kotaro answered confidently.

"Banirra."

Following a stubbornly resisted bout with compulsory Spanish in primary school, my opinion had been pretty much that if anyone had anything worthwhile to say, they would say it in English. Sensei, though, had a knack that I would later come to realize he shared with all gifted teachers. He didn't order me to study Japanese with his wife, didn't suggest I get one of the university's Japanese students who visited at the Kotaro household to tutor me. He just made it clear he considered fluency in the language a necessary requirement for training in the bujutsu and that I wouldn't be taken seriously until I did as well. He *expected* it.

The pressures Kotaro Sensei exerted in this indirect way were very traditionally Japanese and they were successful because I wanted so badly to be accepted as a bugeisha of the Yagyu Shinkage ryu. Sensei had only to note that most Westerners, due to diets high in fatty meats, have an unpleasantly rancid odor detectable at once to the Japanese nose and I immediately diverted my afterschool route to the university gym to shower before going on to the dojo. I scoured myself to a chafed pink with the gym's industrial soap to avoid the *bata kusai*, "butter stinker," pejorative I had heard him and other Japanese use sometimes in describing Westerners. Unconsciously, I adopted the same kinds of conforming behavior the bushi were subjected to in their feudalism. It was the same kind of conforming that would lead them to slit open their bellies rather than risk disappointing their masters.

My daily practice remained centered around the bokken. I attacked invisible enemies, splitting them in half with the vertical stroke that began with the sword raised above my head. When I could execute that cut with some accuracy, I moved on to the diagonal strokes and the more powerful horizontal slashes of the Yagyu style that started at waist level and were driven like a home run hitter's swing with the force of the hips. Through thousands of repetitions, I progressed slowly in the basics of kenjutsu: footwork, rhythm, and timing. Cut, step forward, cut. Turn, cut, cut.

Turn, cut, turn. Whatever Sensei's directions, I could move, my arms and legs starting and stopping at the same instant as my sword. I grew more efficient at clenching my abdominal muscles to let them do the work. According to Yagyu teaching, the arms would make a sword *hit*, while the mass of the hips and abdominal muscles would *cut*, all the way through the target. In every lesson, the emphasis was on delivering a clean blow capable of killing instantly. I was learning to do it and I soon came to fancy myself quite a swordsman.

Then Sensei took me into the backyard where he had set up an old automobile tire fixed to a wooden frame, with the top of the tire about waist level. Sensei explained that swinging a sword in the air was fine for practicing correct motion, but without the actual contact of the sword striking a resilient object, a bugeisha could never develop the strength to make a cut that would be able to cleave an opponent at one stroke. When I first struck down at the tire, I had the sensation that an electrical current was running through it, traveling up the length of my bokken and into me. My wrists had once ached with the effort of learning the cut, but now, when I applied it against the hard rubber, I flinched as a reverberating shock stung from my fingertips to the deepest muscles of my shoulders. I had to be tutored all over again in making the correct body actions: sinking my hips and keeping knees and elbows flexible in order to take the concussive lash that came back when I chopped against the tire.

Under the pewter skies of November, starlings wheeled from the wind, searching for the flock with which they would roost at night and paying no attention to the whacking sounds of the worn tire absorbing my blows. The splashy oranges and scarlets of autumn faded to a resigned brown. Leaves fell around me, gathering in heaps in Mrs. Kotaro's iris beds, defying her attempts to keep them out. At last, she gave in and even helped, mounding them against the sides of the beds as protection from the coming cold.

Sensei's insistence on a thorough understanding of the basics of swordsmanship was well-founded. My legs were toughened by the hours of churning up and down the dojo floor, and when practicing outside I could feel my feet gripping the cold ground underneath them, melding muscle and bone into an extension of the earth when the sword cut. My body hardened.

My mind, too, underwent a change. It wasn't anything like arrogance. If ever I showed the slightest inclination toward becoming, as the Japanese adage goes, "a nail sticking up from the roof," Kotaro Sensei was there to pound me back into place. The change in my attitude came as an inkling sense of meaning I found in the monotonous movements of the Yagyu style of fencing that germinated in me a little at a time under Sensei's watchful guidance. My bujutsu skills were to be an added attraction to me, as I had it figured—another of my prized things, like my French running shoes and my plastic inflatable chair. They weren't, of course. The practice was boring (even more so, in retrospect, than those damnable Spanish lessons in fifth grade), Sensei was frequently harsh and distant, and neither girls nor happiness seemed threatening to smother me just because I was spending each afternoon smacking the hell out of a four-ply radial. Yet increasingly, I was compelled to continue.

My involvement in the bugei in no small way set me apart from many of my friends who were caught up in the social maelstrom of the sixties, flung from protests at the war in Vietnam to the alluring refuge of drug experimentation to the dizzying euphoria of dances and drinking parties—all of which were features of high school life then. For others, those years might have been reddened with the hate for an unjust war or blurred by the vertigo of a pharmacopoeia of recreational chemistry, but for my generation, too young to be drafted, too old to be shielded from all that was deliciously new, the sixties were a crazy kaleidoscope of image and sensation. It was the mad modness of Carnaby Street fashions, the far-outness of Woodstock ("and there were guys and girls right on the news, swimming in a pond, *naked*"); it was frayed jeans, incense, beads and headbands, and hair. It was the burnt rope pungence of marijuana, pizza's biting spice, the metal clash of rock music.

Although a marvelously exciting time to be squeezing out of childhood's shell into the dangerous freedom of the unknown, it was not idyllic. Along with the glamor and glitter of the new, there was that which was threatened merely for being old. In the opinions of my classmates, the meaningful and worthwhile could often be sacrificed wholesale for the chic. Being "with it" was regarded as vital, though "it" was largely undefinable. Nothing was so passé as yesterday's items. Last season was nostalgia; last year, ancient history.

The classical swordsmanship of the Yagyu ryu was hardly modern, and having to conform to ways considered obsolete a century before I was born couldn't very well complement the popular dictum of doing one's own thing. Yet perhaps because of my family roots, sunk into the granite bordered fields of Massachusetts with all their staid and enduring neatness, I felt no hard tugging toward unconvention. A New England identification with the past steered me away from that and into the realm of the bugei of old Japan. The inherited Puritan sense of discipline kept me there despite every shift of fad and fashion the sixties had to offer.

Like most of my adolescent peers, I devoted much of my high school years to finding out what I wanted for myself. I wasn't sure what that was going to be, but between November's frosts and December's snows, somewhere around the one hundred thousandth crack I took at the furrowed tread of the Firestone, I decided the place to look for it was going to be in the dojo of Kotaro Ryokichi of the Yagyu Shinkage ryu.

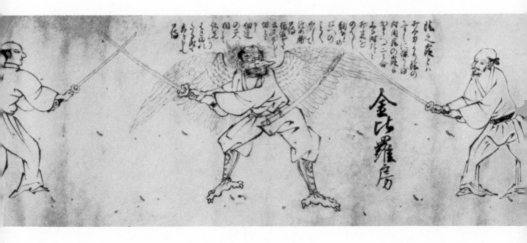

An illustration from the Heihokadensho, *recounting the transmission of secret techniques of the Yagyu school by a* tengu, *or winged mountain goblin.*

6.

The Swordsmen in the Shadows

Between Nara, the ancient capital of Japan, and the immensity of Lake Biwa stands a range of mountains intimidating in their steepness and in their solitude. They are not especially lofty; the Japanese Alps of central Honshu tower over them by at least a thousand feet, but the mountains of the Kinki region along the border between Nara and Kyoto Prefectures instill a sense of awe in the visitor nonetheless. Their quiet dignity emanates from the forests that cover their nearly perpendicular sides. These shadowed stands of cryptomeria, maple, and pine form a barrier of thick green against the outside world.

The mountains are the Kasuga range, a clump of craggy peaks formally nameless except for Mt. Wakakusa to the south, on the edge of Nara, and Mt. Kasagi, the tallest of them. In size and climate they are remarkably similar to the Catskills of southern New York. Along the Kasuga valleys the green is interrupted by the silver ribbon of the Kizu River and there are brief stretches of road—once cobblestone, now asphalt—not concealed by the tunnels of foliage over them. For the most part, however, the predominance of the forest carpet is broken only by an occasional castle or mansion roof rising above the treeline.

In the eons before man kept a record of his doings, the wild Kinki region was the home of mythological creatures. *Kappa*—water dwelling sprites, with the body of a boy encased in a turtle's shell—paddled the swift streams, waiting to leech onto unsuspecting victims and suck the life from them. Winged, pencil-nosed goblins known as *tengu* prowled the mountainous slopes and held animated conferences in boulder-rimmed amphitheaters where they discussed matters of great importance to their kind. And all about, in trees and stones and animals, resided the spirit deities of Shinto, the kami, or gods, who were able to aid their worshippers or to destroy them.

The first human inhabitants of the Kinki area came there as tenants with a healthy respect for their mythic landlords. Along with their huts and grain fields, they erected stone cairns to demonstrate their respect for the beings who were never far away, hovering in the cool high air, lurking behind the gnarled trunk of a giant pine, waiting in the depths of a stream.

By the time of the Taika Reforms in 645, when the Imperial Prince Tenchi and his generalissimo, Fujiwara no Kamatari, were remodeling the Japanese government after the Chinese system, the residents of the Kinki region had come to terms with the deities and spirits of their mountains. Isolated from the reformation that revised much of the rest of the country, they went about their modest business of raising rice, barley, and tea. The larger families gathered into clans that homesteaded on cleared meadows in the mountains. One, the Kambe settlement, eventually became a village, though in comparison with nearby Nara, with its gridded streets and gilded temples, the collection of wattled huts could hardly even be considered an outpost.

For centuries the land of the settlement had been held by the Kambe clan, but it was legally controlled by the Kasuga Taisha

Shrine of Nara, famous for its three thousand lanterns. Early in the fourteenth century, the Shinto priests of the Kasuga Shrine appointed a local Kinki family to supervise their land. The family they chose called themselves Yagyu. A few years after their appointment, the Yagyu found themselves in actual ownership of the land when the shogun in Kamakura, displeased with the Kasuga Shrine priests for some reason, took away their claim and awarded the property to the Yagyu family.

The Yagyu took their appointment as custodians and later as owners of the land quite seriously. Although they were of the same common stock as their peasant neighbors, the Yagyu, according to tales reverently passed down from generation to generation, were descended from the renowned poet and exiled martyr of the Heian era (794-1190), Michizane Sugawara. With a sense of duty sprung from these noble roots, they began to train themselves in the ways of the warrior, lest they be called upon to defend their holdings from invaders. They were a well-armed and highly skilled force of fighters by 1331, when the Emperor Go Daigo fled from his own government in Kamakura to take refuge on Mt. Kasagi, the tallest of the Kasuga range. The Yagyu watched anxiously as the resultant Genko Rebellion boiled around them. Warfare did not touch the Kinki region or the lands of the Yagyu family, however. The Kamakura Shogunate fell, to be replaced by the military family of the Ashikaga, who reigned in peace for nearly two hundred years.

In what was by then a proper little village named Yagyumura, the Ashikaga Period was marked by the passing of seasons that unfolded with a comfortable regularity surpassing the memory of its oldest citizen. With the chill of spring came the planting of the tender emerald rice seedlings, and for weeks, the hands and feet of every peasant would be chalky and cracked from hours of submersion in the sapping cold of the paddy mud. With the summer's heat, the peasants moved up the hillsides to the cleaner work of caring for the tea bushes. Long humid nights were enlivened by ghost stories ages-old of bushi come back from the dead for revenge, or of cats able to transform themselves into men, or of witches, the same hags who figured in folktales on the other side of the earth, who worked their evil magic on the hapless.

In the autumn the villagers of Yagyumura cut wood and—provided the typhoons were merciful when they swept across Japan in September—harvested the rice crop that would sustain them through the winter.

The winters of the Kinki region were not so harsh as those farther north, but they were characterized by huge amounts of snowfall. Houses were buried to the eaves of their thatched roofs and whole trees disappeared under a mantle of white that so immobilized village activity that inhabitants were reduced to spending most of the day huddled around the hearths, repairing farming equipment and dreaming of the warmer days to come.

Taxes were paid annually when an emissary from Nara came with his square wooden measure to take the rice owed. Other than that, the only visitors to Yagyumura were the occasional Buddhist priests on pilgrimages to one of the area's shrines.

The average lifespan in Yagyumura was no longer than anywhere else in Japan then, about forty-five years, but it is safe to say that few villagers expired prematurely from overexcitement.

The Yagyu family turned out to be good supervisors. They built Koyagyu, a mansion on a hill that overlooked the main part of the village. Because they were an integral in community life, they understood the farmer's problems and their administration was fair, continuing without incident all through the fourteenth and fifteenth centuries.

As an extension of the central Imperial government, the Yagyu were relieved of most of the responsibility of supporting themselves directly. They took their allotment of rice, a medium of exchange equally as negotiable as the silver and gold that were also used in business transactions, from the farmers under their control. Freedom from labor in the fields provided the Yagyu with the opportunity to concentrate their energies on the development of their martial arts, a craft they took to with furious enthusiasm. Their mansion contained a roomy dojo for the practice of kenjutsu and soon, besides the tax collector and the itinerant priests who hiked up the cobblestone highway to Yagyumura, the hamlet was visited by traveling martial artists seeking to further their abilities at Koyagyu. In the last decade of the fifteenth century the head of the Yagyu clan, Yagyu Ieyoshi, brought a fencing master of the Tomita school all the way from the cold of northern Echigo Province to instruct, and guests seeking to further their skills at the Koyagyu dojo found it harder and harder to keep up with the swordsmen of Yagyumura.

That the ruling Ashikaga regents were able to maintain the peace as long as they did was a noteworthy accomplishment considering the state of affairs in Japan during those days. For too long, daimyo, bred to battle as a natural part of their lives, were kept in check, prevented from making forays into the increasingly attractive lands of their neighbors. Old feuds were suppressed and scores left unsettled. Bushi grew restless training with no chance of putting themselves to the test of combat. Under such pressures, the control of the Ashikaga faltered. At first it was challenged by a sprinkling of random violence: a warrrior outside his home province drawn into a quarrel with the retainers of another lord that ended with bloodied swords, despite governmental edicts outlawing duels.

The disputes, not uncommon among a class of men who regarded an overly lengthy glance as an invitation to fight, were often tacitly encouraged by daimyo who manipulated the incidents, escalating them into inter-provincial spats. As their ability to quell the petty border warfare declined, the Ashikaga shogun and his court became ever more ineffectual. A series of miniature civil wars broke out, some involving two rival lords with a private matter to settle and others that included participants from several different provinces. Two hundred years were to pass before the warfare finally stopped.

At first, as before, the fighting missed the forested valleys of the Yagyu. The tea bushes continued to sprout dark green leaves that were plucked when they reached the size of a fox's ear, to be chopped and dried into *bancha*, the most ordinary grade of tea. But in 1541, the tea leaves ripened unmolested by harvest. Miyoshi Chokei, general of a clan from Awa Province, announced that the ancestors of Kizawa Nagamasa, a daimyo whose lands included Kawachi and Yamato Provinces, had perpetrated a grievous wrong on the Miyoshi family, one that could only be righted by battle. Though the Yagyu had no more idea what the wrong was than did anyone else involved, they had little choice. Their village lay within the boundaries of Yamato; their duty was to Kizawa.

Under the leadership of Yagyu Ieyoshi, the bushi of the Kinki district gathered up spears, bows, and their long swords and marched in a snaking line over the highway to Mt. Kasagi to help Kizawa defend the province. They were joined by the bushi of neighboring fiefs, men who lived in close proximity in a geographical sense, but who, separated by the isolating Kasuga peaks, had scant knowledge of each other's strengths and shortcomings on the battlefield. The combination did not prove effective. In a decisive engagement against one of Miyoshi's allies, Tsutsui Junsho, Kizawa was unable to assemble his forces competently and he lost the battle as well as his life.

Yagyu Ieyoshi and his retainers retreated from the slopes of Mt. Kasagi with the assurance that they would be pursued. Not immediately; Tsutsui had other problems, other battles, but eventually he would return to the mountains north of Nara to extract a measure of revenge from the bushi who had taken arms against him. As every warrior realized, it was part of the code.

In Yagyumura, news of the defeat was received and its implications understood even before Ieyoshi and his men returned. Retainers at Koyagyu began the work of fortifying the mansion that took three years to complete. Breastworks to protect the outermost walls and massive wooden shutters with forged iron studs to fit over the frail *fusuma* screens of the mansion's inner house were constructed with deliberate care. Platforms were built as vantage points for archers and, in the village below, bushi and their servants piled layers of dirt against the sides of their modest homes so that only the thatched roofs would burn when the structures were set afire.

The elaborate fortifications weren't a needless gesture. On the 27th day of July, 1544, Tsutsui cantered up the road into Yagyumura with 10,000 troops behind him. Just as Takeda Shingen did two decades later at Minowa Castle, Tsutsui sent his men forth in a series of timed charges that used bowmen, then cavalry, then sword-carrying bushi, then *ashigaru* (the foot soldiers armed with pikes and lances), all to the best advantage. Outnumbered ten to one, the bushi of Yagyu were able to hold off Tsutsui for three long days, enduring terrible losses and surviving largely because the skillfully built defenses of Koyagyu made assault almost suicidal. By the end of the third day, though, Ieyoshi was beaten. Most of his village was smoldering ruins, filling the mountain air with greasy smoke. Many of the fief's ablest warriors lay dead or wounded. Rather than see any more of them slaughtered and his mansion, which had withstood the ferocious barrage with minor damage, destroyed, the head of the house of Yagyu capitulated.

The terms under which Ieyoshi surrendered were simple. They required the Yagyu daimyo and his bushi to recognize Tsutsui as the new governor general of the province and to cease further military activity against him.*

Yagyu Muneyoshi was seventeen years old in 1544 when he stood at the foot of the hill beneath Koyagyu. Though the oath he took along with the rest of his father's retainers nearly choked in his throat, he accepted it without showing any of the anger that surged within him. As the eldest son of Ieyoshi, Muneyoshi's aristocratic pride was nurtured and indulged in the same way most *buke,* or bushi families raised their male children. With the Yagyu's defeat, his haughtiness was crushed and then, more humiliatingly, stifled by the forced allegiance to Tsutsui, a bitter drink for the youth to swallow.

The older Kinki samurai were more philosophical. The odds against them had just been too great, they told one another in consolation. They had done their best and could not be faulted for having failed. Indeed, their stand at Koyagyu was praised by bushi and

---

*For Westerners, the idea that loyalty could be so casually terminated might seem to indicate a short supply of courage on the part of Ieyoshi. Among the bushi, however, loyalty was a concept narrowly defined and limited to one's lord, family, and land. Once Kizawa was dead, Ieyoshi and the Yagyu warriors had no reason to continue their battle except to protect their fief. That accomplished, they had no further quarrel with the Miyoshi family or with the Miyoshi's ally, Tsutsui Junsho. The assurance that the Yagyu bushi would submit to Tsutsui's domination was far from absolute, as shall be seen, but was rather an agreement that both sides would refrain from attacking one another for an honorable length of time—or until one side could find a reasonable rationalization.

peasant alike in central Japan and in truth, the mountain hamlet that was their home was barely affected at all by Tsutsui's new position as governor general of the province. But Muneyoshi saw the sequence of events of 1544 through the eyes of adolescent righteousness. While the fief went about the business of repairing the damage done by Tsutsui's siege, he went each day to the dojo at Koyagyu to train in the Tomita ryu's style of fencing with the fervent hope of some day repairing the honor of the Yagyu name.

Fifteen years later, after his father had died and Muneyoshi had assumed the title of daimyo of Yagyu, he got his chance at redeeming the family's pride. Another ally of the Miyoshi clan, Matsunaga Hisahide, turned on Miyoshi and, without warning, attacked Tsutsui Junsho. Muneyoshi read the rebellion as an opportunity for his clan to take revenge on Tsutsui and regain control of the Kinki region, so he immediately joined his forces with those of Matsunaga's.

Muneyoshi's first battle since the loss at Koyagyu occurred in the winter of 1563 when he and Matsunaga led their bushi against the samurai-monks of Tonomine, a monastery in southern Yamato Province. Although as a commanding officer he was expected to remain in the rear, directing the strategy, the new head of the Yagyu clan placed himself at the front of the charge to the monastery walls. Traditionally, the *sohei,* or "warrior monks," favored the halberd or a spear with a hooking crossbar near the tip when they fought, weapons they used with frightening skill. Their status as Buddhist clergymen in no way compromised their warriorship (many of them were actually samurai who had retired from service to a cloistered life); Muneyoshi became painfully aware of their warrior skills as his troops drew nearer to the monastery. The muscles of his arms threatened to cramp for want of rest, yet as soon as one of the sohei fell, another appeared to take his place. Their polearms cut and thrust at him from constantly changing angles, the shafts clacking against his lacquered chest armor as they missed connecting and penetrating just barely.

The movement reached the limen of his attention. Occupied with the task of staying alive in the midst of the sohei, he glanced up to see an archer loose an arrow at him from a gap in the monastery wall. Like many of the kenjutsu ryu devoted to methods of swordsmanship on the battlefield, the Tomita style included techniques of *ya-dome*, "arrow blocking" and Muneyoshi was well-schooled in them. He raised his sword to intercept the arrow's flight instinctively, but the demands of the fight had been too much. His timing was thrown off by his weariness and the arrow struck him squarely in the fist which grippped his sword. With blood spurting from his hand, he was forced to retreat, leaving the fray for his troops to finish.

Even so, Yagyu Muneyoshi left Tonomine with the satisfaction of having taken his revenge. Matsunaga won the battle and, in gratitude for the help supplied by the Yagyu clan, he presented Muneyoshi with a letter describing his heroism and gave him permission to retain complete control of Yagyumura and the lands around it.

Yagyu Muneyoshi's heartless revenge against the Miyoshi clan was typical of the warriorship of his day but it was only one side of the complicated and enigmatic swordsman's personality. Unlike all too many bushi of the Age of Warring Provinces, Muneyoshi was not of a single, compassionless dimension. The accounts of his early years reveal him to have been a highly strung and emotional child. As a swordsman of the rapidly rising Yagyu family, he naturally could not allow his feelings to steer him away from the path of the samurai, so in order to equip himself mentally for his profession he began to place a different emphasis on the training he did in the Koyagyu dojo.

Where most bugeisha sought only to perfect their physical techniques, Yagyu Muneyoshi, while still in his teens, found swordsmanship to be a means of quieting his fears and inner doubts. Instead of practicing a cut only to achieve proficiency in it, he would remain in the dojo long after his lessons were done, repeating again and again the movement he had been taught, losing himself to it until his consciousness was consumed in the action. Then, beyond the ragged breath, under the painful muscles, he discovered a peaceful flowing quiet within the violence of swordsmanship. He had heard only a few stories of the mysterious Kage style of kenjutsu and he knew little more about Kamiizumi Nobutsuna, but through the efforts of his own practice, he was beginning to sense the essence of that ryu: the way of the sword was not in physical techniques, not in victory on the battlefield, but in the realm of the spiritual.

Normally, itinerant bugeisha who stopped in at the Hozoin never even got to see its abbot, Innei. They appeared at the main gate, clanged the iron bell for entrance, and were shown into the small quarters used for visitors to the temple that sat on the crest of Abura Hill, on the southwestern edge of the great city of Nara. When it came time, they were led to a long side yard covered with sand and bordered by a part of the outer temple's whitewashed walls. As challengers to the Hozoin reputation or adepts seeking instruction, they were then met by one of the monks of the temple's lower orders. Sometimes the visitor would be carrying a sword; other times it would be a halberd, or even one of the bugei's more exotic weapons, a length of weighted chain attached to a short pole, or a forked metal truncheon.

Whatever the challenger was wielding, the shaven-headed monk who came out into the courtyard to face him would invariably be armed with a spear, nearly ten feet long and with a crescent bar protruding at right angles a foot or so behind the head. For while other monks in other temples might have been respected for their piety or selflessness, the monks of the Hozoin were famous throughout the land for the nimble skill they displayed (without a second's hesitation) in manipulating their long spears in the way of the Hozoin ryu of *sojutsu*, the spear art.

So the fact that Kamiizumi Nobutsuna and his two disciples were ushered into the main temple and the abbot Innei informed of their arrival was evidence to the monks that this man was no ordinary bugeisha. The three were soon brought to Innei's reception room, where the abbot of Hozo sat reading the letter of introduction Nobutsuna had brought from Kitabatake Tomonori, the governor of Ise Province.

Nobutsuna bowed, concealing his amused surprise at the

abbot's appearance. Innei's robe and plain blue tunic were the same kind worn every day by most members of the Buddhist priest class, but his body was tanned as brown as any farmer's and his legs, bare underneath the short robe and tucked in front of him, were the size of small tree trunks. The fingers that held the letter of introduction were wide and calloused on the sides and looked as though they would be far better suited for gripping a spear than holding a delicate brush for copying sutras.

Innei put the letter down and rubbed his bare head. His eyes sparkled with an inner light that glowed even brighter when he smiled. Those who saw him on the streets of Nara during one of his visits to the city assumed the light was an emanation of the Buddha's joy. Nobutsuna recognized immediately in Innei's flashing glances the look of contented self-confidence radiated by a gifted bugeisha.

"Kitabatake sama is a good friend of mine," Innei was saying, pointing to the signature and seal of Nobutsuna's letter.

"I was pleased to have him as my student for the short time we were in Ise," Nobutsuna replied.

"Ah, Ise." Innei folded his arms across his chest, lost momentarily in memories of that most beautiful of Japanese regions. "How are things there?" he asked.

Nobutsuna shrugged. "The bridge still stands."

Both men laughed. The centuries-old Ujibashi Bridge in front of the Great Shrines of Ise was famous for its sturdy cypress construction which neither incessant use nor the annual spring floods of the Isuzu River below it seemed to endanger. Ujibashi was almost a symbol for permanence and steadfastness.

"Kitabatake sama suggested that a visit here at Hozoin would be a chance to see your respected spear technique," said Nobutsuna politely.

Innei's head bobbed. "I think some of the monks can provide you with an interesting session. None of them have your experience in actual combat, of course. Actually," he added, "I'd like to ask another acquaintance of mine to come and meet you. He's a young swordsman from a village north of here, Yagyumura."

"One of Yagyu Ieyoshi's sons?"

"The youngest," returned Innei. "He's distinguished himself in more than one battle and he has some unusual ideas about swordsmanship. I would like to see how they work against the techniques of your Kage ryu."

Nobutsuna agreed and excused himself to prepare for his exercise with the seniormost of the Hozoin spearmen, the only martial artists at the temple who would be worthy adversaries for him.

The contests between the swords of the Kage ryu and the spears of the Hozoin style were spirited, for the monks were accomplished, probably, Nobutsuna concluded after watching the first match between one of them and his student Hikida, the best spearmen in Japan. Against Hikida and Jingo's bokken, the monks used wooden spears with the tips bound up into a soft leather ball that minimized the chance of accidental injury. When taking a stance, they held their weapons pointing lower to the ground than was customary in most schools of sojutsu. This, Nobutsuna noted, did not leave them open to attack as it might have looked. Instead, it was a ploy to induce their opponents into making a strike to their upper body. As soon as the attack began, the spear would dart up, searching for a spot underneath the opponent's arm. The monks were especially adept at finding this point, jabbing their spears into the folds of the kimono or jacket and twisting with their shoulders and hips, using the spear as a fulcrum to throw the opponent forcefully to the ground.

The Hozoin ryu technique was one both Jingo and Hikida quite literally fell for. Each in turn thought he saw the obvious weakness in the monk's stance and no sooner had he begun his overhead blows than he found himself sitting on the ground and brushing sand from his clothes.

Nobutsuna, however, wary from his exposure to battle, did not try to take advantage of the Hozoin ryu's peculiar stance. In response, he lowered his bokken and advanced in measured, crossing steps aimed at bringing himself as close as possible to offset the spear's superior length. His sandals made a dry hissing sound on the sand. When he had drawn within range, Nobutsuna became the target of a monk who made a sudden slashing motion toward his opponent's knee. Had the spear carried a sharp steel blade and had it connected, the edge would have sliced through the leg of the Kage ryu fencer, crippling him. It was such a powerful and dangerous cut that many bugeisha would involuntarily flinch away as soon as they saw it begin. Nobutsuna, however, had used the same technique at the siege of Minowa and he recognized it now as merely a feint.

Without a pause, the monk switched his method of attack, moving in, twirling the spear in a circular motion intended to deflect Nobutsuna's bokken and allow a stab at his chest. Only too late did he realize that the swordsman was no longer holding his bokken pointing downward. Before he could pull back from his charge, Nobutsuna jumped forward, scissoring his legs in midair to keep himself close to the ground and raising his bokken in front of his face. As he landed, he struck with the overhead cut of the Kage style, stopping it an inch from the monk's forearms.

"Sooo," sighed the monk unhappily. He retreated a few paces and bowed, thanking Nobutsuna for the lesson which, had both men been armed with real weapons, would have ended with his blood gushing into the sand.

Although he was clearly beaten, the monk-spearman's dismay was short-lived. Mock duels such as the kind he and Nobutsuna engaged in were almost a daily occurrence in his training in sojutsu and his loss was perceived mainly as just another lesson. If Nobutsuna had come to the Hozo temple after making disparaging remarks about the Hozoin ryu or to settle a grudge against one of the monks, the fight would have had a much more serious tone and the outcome would have been considerably more violent, as was attested to by those of the Hozoin clergy who walked with a limp or a permanently disfigured limb, as well as by the cemetery in the temple compound containing the remains of less fortunate challengers. As it was, Nobutsuna congratulated his opponent on his talents with the spear and then offered some advice on how he might improve his sojutsu tactics so that he would fare better when he met another swordsman who used Nobutsuna's methods. Theirs was a battle between civilized warriors.

An ordinary practice match could be turned into a more serious occasion when two bugeisha of reputation (it mattered little whether earned or not) fought one another. Even though the encounter was still technically only a practice using blunted or wooden substitutes, victory and defeat were of crucial importance. In sixteenth century Japan, the good name and quality of his ryu determined much of the bugeisha's status and respect, so the struggle for superiority was fierce among the best of them. It was one thing for a spear fighting monk to be beaten by a famous master swordsman like Kamiizumi Nobutsuna, for instance. It would be quite another for a man of Yagyumura, the best known fencers in the whole of Nara Province, to find defeat against the swordsman of any ryu.

The furry-needled branches of the cryptomeria groves atop Abura Hill were still green, but on the boughs of the elm-like zelkova, the leaves were tinged with yellow and some had already fallen on the grounds of Hozoin. In the same kind of autumn two years earlier, Nobutsuna remembered while he sat under the temple eaves, he had surrendered at Minowa. During the intervening seasons, he and Hikida and Jingo had traveled over much of central Japan, testing the techniques of the Kage school against dozens of bugeisha. If those they met were worthy enough, Nobutsuna would take up the bokken. That he had not yet been beaten was already sparking rumors that had been told of Kage ryu swordsmen for some time: that they were the possessors of some secret techniques or mysterious abilities that rendered them indomitable.

Nobutsuna wondered if the man sitting so erectly at the edge of the Hozoin practice yard feared such a secret power. If so, he did not show it. Yagyu Muneyoshi waited in the bright autumn sunshine, his legs tucked beneath him on the clean tatami that was laid down in preparation for the match. From his rough-soled sandals to his casually tied topknot, he was typical in appearance of a country lord's son. His manner, shy and polite but lacking in affectation, was equally indicative of his rural, aristocratic upbringing.

He had come to the temple the night before. After sharing a simple meal of pickles and rice with the abbot Innei, Nobutsuna, and the other two Kage ryu disciples, he had formally asked Nobutsuna for a lesson in swordsmanship. When Nobutsuna assented,

Muneyoshi excused himself to retire early. It was possible, Nobu-tsuna decided, that the young fencer from Yagyumura was attempting to gain a psychological advantage by his quiet, almost standoffish behavior. If so, it was an advantage soon to be lost.

Nobutsuna gestured for Hikida to accompany him. He emerged from the shadow of the temple eaves with Hikida at his side and approached Muneyoshi, who stood immediately and bowed to the master swordsman.

"Yagyu san. Since you've requested a lesson, I believe you'll find my student Hikida Bungoro to be a most competent teacher. He will meet you now."

Muneyoshi bowed again. He had expected a match with the master himself, of course, but by the polite wording of his request the night before, he had placed himself in the position of a student asking for instruction, so naturally he could hardly question Nobu-tsuna's decision. Thwarted by his own good manners, Muneyoshi knew there was nothing to do but accept the circumstances philosophically. He did not believe the gossip that the Kage school possessed magical properties. His training at the dojo and on the battlefield had taught him that winning in combat depended upon one's presence of mind and an attitude of fearlessness and he was confident of his own skills. Whatever the Kage style had to teach him, he would find out soon enough.

Muneyoshi, armed with a bokken, saw that Hikida was not. Hikida, noticing the look his strange weapon received from Muneyoshi, explained as the two stood together on the sand, oblivious to the crowd watching them intently from a distance.

"It's an invention of my master's he calls a *fukuro shinai,*" he said, holding it up for Muneyoshi's inspection. Hikida's weapon was of the same length and weight as a normal bokken; but it was straight, a cylinder of wood covered with layers of cloth padding and bound up in a leather sheath.

"Because of the padding," continued Hikida, "it's possible to make contact in a match without injury."

Muneyoshi examined the sword carefully and he felt a sudden admiration for Nobutsuna. In practices with the bokken, he had seen even highly trained swordsmen sometimes lose fractional control of their weapons, resulting in accidents that were often crippling. With the fukuro shinai, a fully unleashed blow might raise a nasty bump or bruise, but the chance of significant damage was slight. In addition, the shinai permitted a fencer to be sure that he was delivering his attacks with the proper focus and energy.

Muneyoshi handed the shinai back to Hikida. Both bowed and assumed postures, Muneyoshi holding his bokken pointing straight out in the *chudan kamae* (middle level posture) while Hikida lifted his shinai up so that its tip was aimed directly at his opponent's eyes. After only a few moments of maneuvering to feel each other out, Muneyoshi was absolutely sure of one thing. Hikida's loss to the Hozoin spearman, he decided, was undoubtedly due to Hikida's deliberately providing an opening in his defenses to test the spearman's strike. The defeat was not a fault in Hikida's prowess; in all his dojo and battle experience, Muneyoshi had never come up against a warrior of such overwhelming power.

Seated in the shadows of the temple's wide porch next to Nobutsuna, the abbot Innei came to the same conclusion, at the same time as Muneyoshi. "This is not the same man who lost to the monk Nomura yesterday," he said to Nobutsuna without taking his eyes off the two men in the practice yard.

Nobutsuna smiled. Both Hikida and Jingo had purposely let the Hozoin spearmen attack and defeat them. Then, Nobutsuna, armed with the newly gained knowledge of Hozoin ryu techniques, was able to counter them in his own match. "You've heard the stories, haven't you?" he retorted teasingly. "We of the Kage ryu are a mysterious lot." It was Innei's turn to grin, and the two resumed their concentration on the match unfolding before them.

Muneyoshi knew he was in trouble from the beginning. Fat beads of perspiration were gathered at his hairline, the result of strenuous mental exertions. Hikida barely shifted his feet at all in response to Muneyoshi's feints and tentative thrusts. His padded sword never wavered.

"To win or lose is not important," Muneyoshi was telling himself. "Think of the breathing." It was a strategy that had allowed him to overcome every other opponent of his career, concentrating on his own exhalations until his subconscious took over and guided his inevitably perfect attack. Now, under Hikida's stare, it failed him. Twice, then three times he started to raise his bokken in an attempt to make Hikida move and expose a weakness, but the Kage ryu disciple never budged other than to pivot his body so that he was constantly facing Muneyoshi.

"Go, go . . . . Now!" Muneyoshi's limbs refused to obey his brain's commands. Hikida was just too perfectly composed, too controlled in his every motion, to permit an attack to be made against him. For less than a second, Muneyoshi was distracted, wondering just for an instant how he would defeat Hikida if his usual approach was not going to work.

Hikida's shinai went from a position of motionlessness to a flickering snap as the Yagyu fencer ducked in a stumbling effort to avoid the blow. His adrenalin pumping at a gushing rate, Muneyoshi at first thought Hikida's strike had missed him. He straightened, shook his shoulders, and resumed his posture with the bokken outward, intent on continuing the match. Then again Hikida struck with the same sureness as before and Muneyoshi felt the sting of the shinai's leather as it cracked on the same spot it had hit before, squarely on the middle of his forehead.

For perhaps the only time in his adult life, all the composure of a rugged and stoic Kinki upbringing fled Muneyoshi the bugeisha. The bokken slipped from his grasp and his chin fell forward to his chest, his shoulders slumping. A pitiful moan escaped from somewhere inside him. He realized that his painstakingly wrought ideas on the nature of his art were flawed—that, in fact, they might have gotten him killed. He was a man who saw in a flash of illumination that his victories in swordsmanship had not been because of any great insight on his part, but because of ordinary skill and a generous helping of luck. In his misery, he did not even notice that Nobutsuna had come up to stand beside him.

"Here, Muneyoshi." Nobutsuna picked up the dropped bokken and handed it to Muneyoshi, who looked up with puzzlement. "Now," said the master of the Kage style, "I will be your opponent."

Why the teacher of the one who had so completely defeated

him would want a match was beyond Muneyoshi, but he was enough of a samurai to regain control of himself and he bowed. Again he held his sword in the middle posture he had taken so successfully so many times, and Nobutsuna, holding Hikida's shinai, directed his weapon at Muneyoshi's face, just as Hikida had done. Their gazes met and Muneyoshi stared into fathomless eyes that seemed to draw the strength from his arms. Once again he told himself to concentrate, but this time, still feeling the slap of the shinai on his head, he could not ignore the futility of continuing the duel. Nobutsuna was looking into his very soul and he was defenseless. At least he could save himself from appearing a fool. He retreated a few paces and crouched on his knees, bowing fully to Nobutsuna.

"You are my superior in every way," said Muneyoshi, his voice trembling. "I can go no further in my pursuit of swordsmanship without your help."

Nobutsuna returned the salutation. His evaluation of Muneyoshi, begun the moment he saw the young fencer struggle against Hikida, was complete. The son of the lord of Yagyumura was not as technically proficient as he could be, but that was a matter of lacking the best instruction and could soon be remedied. In Muneyoshi's eyes Nobutsuna saw something difficult to describe, yet which he understood utterly and appreciated as only a master of his level could. Within Yagyu Muneyoshi were qualities waiting to be brought out and polished, qualities that were at the heart of the Kage ryu's philosophy of fencing. Though Muneyoshi had been beaten for the first time by the Kage school, Nobutsuna suspected that he was well on his way to perfecting its innermost virtues.

"Will you accept me as a student?" asked Muneyoshi.

"Yoshii," replied Nobutsuna. "All right."

7.
A Ritual of Style, A Function of Grace

The twentieth-century painter Andrew Wyeth was reminiscing once about the introduction to art his father, N. C. Wyeth, had given him. The elder Wyeth, a renowned illustrator, had insisted that Andrew spend hour upon hour in the basics of painting and drawing, learning to use the charcoal stick and watercolor brush to perfect on paper the vagaries of shape and shadow. He was rarely allowed to experiment or to deviate from the strict guidelines set by his father. Years after he had become the internationally famous painter he is today, Wyeth recalled his father's words when he was asked if the rigid education might not have threatened to kill the emerging genius and creativity of the young painter.

"If it kills it, it ought to be killed," N. C. said.

His son now agrees. "If it isn't strong enough to take the gaff of real training, then it's not worth very much."

I took the sword rather than the pencil or brush as my tool, but my training was no less severe than Wyeth's. For me, like all bugeisha, the demanding basics of my craft were taught by the exercises of *kata*.

The Japanese character for kata means "shape" or "form." A vertical stroke with the sword, a horizontal slash, or a lunging thrust are all kinds of *waza*, or techniques, but when they are combined in a special way as a series of predetermined blocks, attacks, and counterattacks, they become kata. To the observer, kata might look like a form of dance, choreographed movement with a stiff ritualism far removed from the spontaneity of real combat. The dazzling speed and apparently instinctive displays of swordsmanship of the samurai in the Japanese movies I had watched were a far cry from the step, cut, drop to one knee, and block routine that Kotaro Sensei taught me. I thought the action contrived, even when he assumed the role of my opponent. I imagined a dozen places where I might alter the kata and make a successful attack against him.

The first kata of the Yagyu Shinkage ryu required me to step forward four times, delivering an overhead strike, then a sideways slash from left to right, followed by a reverse cut from right to left, and finishing with a stab to the chest. The defender in this kata moves steadily backward in response to the assaults, blocking and redirecting the assailant, countering the final thrust with a slicing cut that would sever the arms of the attacker if the weapons were not of wood. As I repeated the sequence to memorize it, Sensei simply met my oaken blade, assuming the role of the defender and putting nothing of the tremendous strength of his hips and shoulders into the blocks. When we had covered the length of the dojo floor, we switched roles and slowly waltzed back again, this time with him attacking, again without force, and me defending.

As I began to learn them, the kata of the Yagyu style of swordsmanship had none of the speed and force of the individual techniques I performed daily. But patiently, Sensei increased the tempo of the two man exercises. His blocks came a little bit faster, with more focus. In attacking, his speed was even greater. I hardly finished making one parry before the second cut was upon me, forcing me back steadily. The difference between cutting and de-

78

fending against an imaginary opponent or my tire, and entering a session with another body that moved and struck back was enormous. I would find myself skipping in an effort to keep up with my teacher as he retreated ever more quickly from the reach of my bokken. When I did catch up, I would be out of place for the following strike and Sensei's bokken would come down like a lash on my hands or wrists. The return trip up the dojo floor was just as swift, with Sensei's hacking cuts constantly threatening. Where once I had been able to make a strong stance and creditable block, I found myself batting with my bokken and scrambling to avoid getting hit.

Under the pressure of the kata, attention was narrowed. My mind was filled with the sounds of the dojo, the slap, shuffle, slap of our feet as they slid across the smooth wooden planks; the sharp bark of the bokken meeting; the rustling of hakama; my labored pants—and the steady, overwhelming hiss as Sensei exhaled, always exhaled, like a tiger approaching from the forest.

Breathing correctly—in combat and in everyday life—is a matter of concern to all martial artists. According to ryu scrolls passed down through generations of bugeisha, breathing was a key to expertise in all the warrior arts as well as in other disciplines, from swordsmithery to calligraphy. In these crafts, intricate work is usually performed during exhalation, which is often accompanied by a regulating chant of some kind. Instructional scrolls from these arts contained explanations of proper breathing techniques, some of them having originated far back in Taoist China, where an individual's breath was intimately connected with his *ki* (*chi* in Chinese), the animating force of life. During inhalation, the old texts maintained, the body is momentarily vulnerable and soft as the ki is in the process of being drawn in and centered. Upon exhaling, especially when the breath is pressed down against the diaphragm, strength in the abdomen is concentrated. The ki extends like an electrical current and one's body is made hard and capable of delivering or withstanding an effective attack. To develop a proper respiration, exponents of the bujutsu use a form of ritual from the Shinto religion for purifying the body and spirit of the worshipper. This ritual is called *misogi*.

Although Sensei only showed me how to perform his method of misogi once, he told me that it would have a strong effect on both my breathing during training and on the cultivation of my spirit, for it was really not a contrived method, but an attempt at returning to the natural respiration of a baby.

"But Sensei," I responded dubiously, "I'm Christian, not Shinto." (Although she never voiced it to me, I believe my mother's gravest worry over my involvement with something as exotic as the bujutsu was that I would be caught up in a kind of weird Oriental cult. The thought of performing a Shinto purification ritual left me uneasy with images of primitive rites and magical incantations.) Kotaro Sensei explained that while misogi had its roots in the Shinto religion, it was later practiced as a form of *seishin tanren*, or "spirit forging," that was devoid of specific religious meaning.

Misogi was a favorite training exercise of the famous swordsman and Zen calligrapher, Yamaoka Tesshu. Yamaoka, who lived through the dying years of feudalism and into Japan's modernization, held to a firm belief that the way of the warrior was one of self-discipline and service to mankind. At Shunpukan, his dojo, all his disciples performed misogi sessions regularly. One of them, Tetsuju Ogura, founded his own dojo later on, and it was there that Kotaro Sensei and many other classical martial artists had attended misogi sessions in the days before the second World War.

Actually, misogi is a term covering many kinds of spiritual purification that are achieved through acts of austere physical hardships, endured with the strength gained by misogi breathing. Some practitioners stand under freezing waterfalls or wade into icy rivers as they chant, cleansing themselves inside and out. The misogi taught by Yamaoka and his descendants called for the bugeisha to begin sitting in seiza, the seated bow, with eyes closed.

"Breathe in for a count of ten," Sensei directed. "Then hold. Press air down, against stomach." I held the chestful of air, counting slowly to five, then began a measured exhale for ten more counts.

"Now hold again, count five." Emptying my lungs completely and then trying to count slowly while breathless was unpleasant, like a self-induced form of suffocation. I had to resist the urge to gulp in the next breath. But if I "kept my feelings low," as Sensei put it, sinking my consciousness into my hara (the lower abdomen from where all my spirit emanated, according to the philosophy of the bugei), I was able to make an improvement in the control of my breathing that regulated it during my practice and other physical activities, and during rest.

After I understood the basics of misogi breathing, Sensei gave me a *suzu*, a small bell that looked like the hand grenades used by the German Army. The suzu was a closed cylinder of light brass with two metal balls inside and a wooden handle protruding out of one end. Grasping the cylinder at the bottom of his fist, Sensei brought the suzu up and down with a vigorous vertical stroke of his arm and it clanged. The intent was to match the bell's ringing with my counting as I breathed. Later, I would add the chant of the misogi adherent, "Toho kami, emi tame, toho kami, emi tame."

The concentration required to keep the bell in time with my breathing and chanting, not to mention the suffering I still felt when forced to sit in the seiza position for long periods, was painful drudgery. Sensei explained that misogi practice with the suzu bell had been much, much harder at the dojo where he had trained, its special session lasting for three continuous days, with students getting little sleep and only a few raw vegetables for nutrition. In addition, misogi had been carried out by the senior members of the dojo, some of whom were assigned to be *kagura*, or assistants. The kagura stalked through the rows of seated bell ringers, battering those who lost their rhythm with lengths of bamboo. At the end of three days, Sensei recalled, his back was beaten to a bruised pulp, he could barely speak beyond a hoarse whisper from the hours of chanting, and he was emotionally drained. But he described the gruelling episode as one in which he had experienced a dramatic breakthrough in his own maturation as a bugeisha.

"Too tired just to use muscles, too tired to think to keep rhythm. Body finished, then spirit takes over. In misogi, you find spirit is stronger. It can take you farther than your mind or your body. After misogi, I saw that just living on the physical level, the mental level, that's no good. Man, woman, we are meant to live on a spiritual level."

It was quite a speech for a man who had spent the last six months in the dojo saying little to me other than "Not too bad, try again." So I continued to practice the methods of misogi breathing on my own. Years later, when playing Rugby or soccer or working very hard at my university studies and feeling the creeping numbness of physical exhaustion, my breathing ragged, from a place in the far corner of my memory's vault I would hear the brassy peal of the suzu and the chant, "Toho kami, emi tame . . ."

Even though the sword was the central arm of the curriculum, most bujutsu ryu taught the use of many of the bushi's weapons. The Yagyu Shinkage style was no exception. In time—probably because he grew bored of my fumbling with the bokken—Kotaro Sensei introduced me to sojutsu, the art of the spear as it was practiced by Yagyu ryu bugeisha. A slightly tapering shaft of wood eight feet long, the *yari*, or spear, is manipulated in an entirely different way than the sword. Thanks to spearmen during the feudal age like Kakuzenbo Innei, abbot of the Hozo Temple and the friend who introduced Yagyu Muneyoshi to Nobutsuna, the yari came to be every bit as efficient a weapon as the sharpest sword.

Under these spearmen's care, the ordinary yari also assumed a wide variety of shapes. According to one legend, Innei was once challenged by a brash young peasant boy who, while he had had only the barest of training in the bujutsu, was of such a strong spirit and determination that Innei became afraid he would be beaten by the youngster. The abbot practiced determinedly in preparation for the match, but his workouts only increased his anxieties. On the night before their duel, Innei was in the temple garden, holding his lance out in contemplation over the edge of the garden pond. He gazed at the weapon's reflection in the water and at that moment, the story goes, a finger of lightning reached out overhead, appearing in the pond's reflection as if it crossed the yari's shaft right under the head. Acting upon this inspiration, Innei hafted onto his spear a short crossbar that greatly increased the yari's effectiveness at blocking or catching an opponent's arm or leg. His new invention dispelled his worries; he slept soundly that night, sure of the morrow's victory.

Whether other spearmen were so inspired or not, they came up with a generous assortment of yari. Some had blades hook-shaped, others had a forked tine at the blade's base to trap an enemy's weapon, and others had barbed shafts for catching at an opponent's garments. No matter how the yari was constructed, however, it was never a projectile in Japan, as it was in other parts of the world. Instead, the bugeisha used the yari to jab and thrust, or to cut and slash, exploiting the spear's long, double-edged blade.

Sensei showed me how a sojutsu exponent could hold a swordsman, or even a group of swordsmen, at bay with the kata of the yari; this included whirling slices and thrusts that came from odd angles and were propelled by the torqueing twist of the spear-man's body. Like Kamiizumi Nobutsuna had done on that long ago afternoon at the Hozoin, I also learned to use the sword against the yari, sidestepping and flicking away the spear's jabs until I could get close enough to make an attack with the shorter weapon.

The sojutsu of the Yagyu school offered a wide range of techniques, both offensive and defensive, but traditionally and practically, the spear's most valuable asset was the single, concen-trated *tsuki*, or thrust, it was capable of delivering. Many Zen mas-ters trained with the yari, because the irreversible commitment of the body that was required in a thrust was analogous to their idea of the firmly committed, never-look-back philosophy that charac-terized Zen itself.

No matter how many techniques I was taught with the spear, Sensei insisted that the basis of my sojutsu practice be in the mas-tering of this thrust. He drew a circle the size of an orange chest high on the trunk of one of the big pines in the backyard and in front of it I stood, battering away at the chalk circle, wondering if the abbot Innei had ever known arms as sore as mine.

The *naginata*, a polearm as long as the yari but with a slightly curved halberd blade at the end, was not only a favorite weapon of some of the bushi and bugeisha who specialized in it, it was also the arm nearly all samurai women were taught to use to defend themselves and their homes in times of invasion. Today, naginatajutsu has evolved into a modern budo form, practiced by girls and women who study it to develop balance, grace, and poise. Since Kaoru, Sensei's wife, was from the Yoshioka family, a venerable samurai clan, and had attended an old fashioned private girl's school in Japan, I knew she had been instructed in the art of the naginata. She had pictures of herself as a coed during the War, posing with her class, their wooden naginata held up beside them. But when I asked her to demonstrate her skills for me, she would only laugh and tell me she was too old for such things. "This my naginata now," she said once, hefting the hoe she used to defend her iris beds from encroaching weeds. Then one day I came to the dojo to find my sensei, bokken in hand, at practice with her.

As I crouched in the doorway, Kaoru was kneeling at the far end of the room, wearing a light, white kimono-like blouse called a *monsuki* and a hakama of the same color. She was in the process of knotting a cord around both her shoulders so that it crossed over in the middle of her back. The silk cord pulled up the flaring sleeves of the monsuki, giving her arms more freedom. When she finished tying it, she picked up the wooden naginata beside her and moved to the center of the floor where Sensei waited.

I was used to seeing Kaoru working in her beloved iris gardens, or fixing meals in the kitchen while attuned to the tiny television there, watching soap operas the plots of which she understood practically nothing, or sitting in the living room, reading and listening to the modern jazz she and Sensei liked so much. She gave me fat little *manju** cakes after school rather than the tollhouse cookies my mother baked. In the months of my bugei training I had come to view her as an only slightly different version of an ordinary American housewife. So it was a surprise for me to watch her glide with a feline sort of grace, a commanding though perfectly feminine strength, through the forms of the naginata. Sensei, as her opponent, matched her tempo, beginning slowly and then stepping up the action.

As they progressed, the kata getting longer and more com-

Manju are pastries filled with sweetened bean paste. They are a popular snack for children and a common votive offering at temples.

plex, Kaoru appeared to be in the eye of some ever more furiously brewing storm. The naginata spun in circles and arcs, flicking up in a cut against her husband's inner thigh and then reversing itself to hack down at his shoulder. I had seen enough of my teacher's mastery to know that he was not exerting all of it, but he was twisting and turning, dodging the halberd's mock blade and jumping into the air to make attacks of his own—attacks which Kaoru nimbly evaded, her hakama swishing, her monsuki crackling as she countered. It was a violent ballet in which a mistake, even though they were using practice weapons, would result in a serious injury at the least. Kaoru stomped her foot, using the momentum to whip the naginata overhead and down in a chop meant to bisect her partner vertically. It struck Sensei's bokken so hard that I winced. Kaoru immediately withdrew as if to retreat a step, but she was actually pivoting around and once again the halberd's edge came slicing, horizontally now, at Sensei's knee. She hissed with the effort of the blow. My master kicked up his endangered leg so that the naginata passed under and then, balanced on the other, he hopped to close the distance and struck, the bokken flashing in a blur toward his wife's head. Both stopped, moved apart, and bowed, and then went on to the next kata.

Her face flushed and her shoulders heaved, but through the whole performance, Kaoru's eyes never changed. They were blacker than ever, deep and expressionless, a haughty, self-confident contemplation polished to a cold luster by a hundred generations of samurai breeding. When they finished the practice, she bowed and left. And I, who believed that the bujutsu were the sole possession of the masculine bugeisha, learned that day that *bushi damashi*, the spirit of the warrior, was not a quality engendered by sex.

With the yari, the naginata, and my sweat-stained bokken, I continued my study of the kata. As I did, I often kept in mind the image of Sensei and Kaoru, their bokken and naginata seeming to be extensions of themselves, moving through a continuum that was no different in form from the same kata done countless times before by previous bugeisha, and yet one in which they transformed the actions into their own manner of private experience. This is what is meant by martial *art*, the forging of a personal statement through the precisely disciplined techniques of the kata.

For the beginner, the kata is only a method of rote memorization. It is a device to learn techniques and to put the motions of combat into a coherent shape. As the bugeisha continues on his way, though, the kata become a finely wrought means of self-expression and a path to go beyond the mundane. I had heard tales of bugeisha in Japan during the latter stages of the second World War, their homes reduced to hovels by the Allied bombings, their diet little more than rice gruel and stale turnips. Yet in the midst of their misery, they achieved an inner peace in the perfection of their kata.

Within the sphere they drew about themselves in their kata, Kaoru and my sensei created their own space, and their movements became the subtlest form of expressing their love, their respect, and their place in the world as they perceived it. By understanding the kata in this light, I began to see what Sensei had told me from the very first about it.

"To perfect the kata," he explained, "is to transcend everyday things. It is to reach *seishi choetsu*, the state beyond life and death."

Wooden statue of Yagyu Munenori (1571–1645), founder of the Yagyu Shinkage ryu.

8.

The Shogun's Master

In April of 1565, the fourth month of the seventh year of Eiroku, when the fuzzy buds on the maples of Yagyu village had swelled to the size of a badger's ear, Kamiizumi Nobutsuna presented his disciple Yagyu Muneyoshi with a certificate of proficiency in what, according to the characters brushed on the fine mulberry parchment, was the Shinkage ryu of kenjutsu.* Although his other two students, Jingo Muneharu and Hikida Bungoro were under Nobutsuna's tutelage longer than Muneyoshi, Nobutsuna was confident that in the swordsman from Yagyu were the qualities of a warrior who would carry on and perhaps even improve the Shinkage ryu.**

*Shin in this instance meant "new" or "reformed." Nobutsuna felt that under his supervision the Kage ryu had been developed and refined to a point that it represented a recognizably distinctive form from the original, and so he added the prefix. Thus, Nobutsuna is considered the founder, or shosei, of the Shinkage ryu and Yagyu Muneyoshi, its first headmaster.

**Hikida and Jingo both continued their training under Nobutsuna and others. Respectively, they later founded the Hikida Kage ryu and the Jingo ryu.

The opinions and beliefs of contemporary bugeisha not-withstanding, the secrets of both the old and new versions of the Kage style of the martial arts were not the results of any super-natural divination, even though for many generations to come, once they had been established as the ablest practitioners of the ryu, the men of Yagyu were to be linked with dealings with the mountain tengu (goblin) spirits. Instead, the Kage and Shinkage ryu's foundation was built on a single guiding principle, which Muneyoshi grasped so completely that there was no question in his master's mind that this student would be granted the title of headmaster of the ryu and initiated into its highest teachings. Drawn from sources in Asia so ancient that no one could possibly have traced their roots, the principle was profound, yet of perfect simplicity. According to the principle, if a man's mind is crowded with the ten thousand incidentals that threaten to hurry their way into our consciousness every moment of life, then inevitably he will find himself concentrating on one or another of them, and at that moment his thoughts—and actions—are stopped. However, if he is able to diffuse his consciousness, allowing every bit of input to pass in without focusing on any, then his mind flows with a con-stancy and celerity that makes his motions utterly spontaneous; ap-propriate. Whether he is drinking a cup of tea or cleaving an enemy's head in half with a sword, he will be in accord with the movements of the universe itself. Of course, when a swordsman kept himself so receptive, his mind calmly centered, then he re-vealed nothing of his mind to an opponent. His strategy was kept hidden, in the shade, so to speak. It was this philosophy that gave the ryu its name and its exponents such awesome reputations as bugeisha.

By the customs of lineage and inheritance within the Japanese martial ryu, Muneyoshi's acceptance of the certificate from Nobu-tsuna made him the successor to the Shinkage ryu's leadership. Under more normal circumstances, the position would have meant that Muneyoshi could have ascended to an honored place as the master teacher of the school, instructing at the dojo at Koyagyu. But once again turmoil swept over Japan and once more the war-riors of Yagyumura felt the effects of its ill winds. Not until more than ten years after he had been given the certificate by Nobutsuna was Muneyoshi able to take his place as full-time headmaster of the ryu, with over a decade spent in so many battles that the formal crest of the Yagyu clan became two linked *jingasa*, the wide, pan-shaped helmets of the samurai.

Summer, 1600, the fourth year of Keicho, and Toyotomi Hideyoshi, the peasant general, the great unifier of Japan, was dead. He surpassed the performance of his former commander.* During his reign, by gifted foresight, sound governmental policy, and—not unimportantly—cunning treachery, he was able to bring to a temporary end the continual warfare that had sputtered and flamed since the days of Takeda Shingen and Uyesugi Kenshin. He thus provided Japan with a prosperous and peaceful interlude that allowed samurai to tend their wounds and polish their swords. It was a time altogether too brief.

Part of Hideyoshi's success was due undoubtedly to his willingness to share administrative authority with a *go-tairo*, a council of five regents selected from among the most influential or wealthy of the daimyo. With his death, however, the halcyon seasons were threatened: almost immediately the council of regents split into two irreconcilable factions—those who supported a continuation of Toyotomi rule through Hideyoshi's son Hideyori, and those who advocated naming the politically strongest member of the council, Tokugawa Ieyasu, as shogun, the military governor of Japan.

All through a torpidly hot summer the two sides wrestled in a subtle, vastly intricate contest for control of the country. Discreetly worded inquiries were sent to lesser but strategically vital daimyo in an effort to discern where their sympathies would lie at the outbreak of war. The replies were equally guarded as everyone joined

*Oda Nobunaga (1513-1582) started the task of bringing Japan under a central leadership, but his rule was marked by cruel despotism. He was finally murdered by one of his own generals, creating a vacancy that allowed Hideyoshi to seize power. Interestingly, while both Hideyoshi and Nobunaga were considerably successful during their reigns, neither could legally assume the coveted title of shogun—that august office was restricted, by ancient Imperial decree, to those who could trace their heritage to the Minamoto family.

the waiting, watching to see which group would gain the upper hand before revealing their own plans. It was as though the leaders of the two factions, the wizened little Tokugawa and the portly Ishida Mitsunari, were involved in a nationwide version of the board game of *go*, played as always, with measured caution and infinite, finely tuned patience.

Tokugawa Ieyasu, originally an ally of Nobunaga's who had deferred to the authority of Hideyoshi reluctantly, was unquestionably the underdog in the match. Through the strength of his personality and his reputation he had won many over to his side, but he was also fully aware that the daimyo were men of tradition and that instinctively, their support was for the rightful heir, Hideyoshi's son. Tokugawa was faced then with the tricky problem of having to depend upon allies of fragile loyalty. His rival, Ishida Mitsunari, on the other hand, had the support of more daimyo and the full weight of the Toyotomi family's claim.

Finally, in August the prepatory maneuvering and planning came to an end. A pro-Toyotomi regent, Uyesugi Kagekatsu, began raising an army in his home province, making it clear that his target was Tokugawa, whom he accused of treason. At the same time, Ishida Mitsunari tipped his hand, leading an army of samurai with the intent of catching Tokugawa in a pincer between himself and Kagekatsu.

Ishida's plans were so well laid and timed that it looked as if Tokugawa was headed for certain defeat, and except for two craftily engineered stratagems unleashed at precisely the right moments, he would have been. First of all, Tokugawa gave every impression that he was ready, even eager, for a fight. Earlier in the summer he had left his castle in Osaka, paused at another residence, Fushimi, and then diverted his army to his stronghold, the marshy, mosquito-ridden city of Edo, where he grouped his forces and waited. Back at Fushimi Castle, however, between himself and the advancing enemy, Tokugawa left a core of seasoned samurai—led by his most trusted general—to stop Ishida and foil the pincer.

The castle defense of Fushimi was merely a stalling measure though. Tokugawa knew that eventually he would be unable to avoid meeting in battle Ishida and perhaps many other Toyotomi regents. Further, he had a good idea that the battlefield would be somewhere in central Japan, not far from the steep mountains and deep forests of the Kinki district, the home of the Yagyu clan as well as several other minor nobles. If his guess was correct, it would be absolutely vital to have the help of those daimyo. As it happened, Tokugawa had no real allies among the Kinki lords, but in his service was a young man whose father was the most powerful of them all. Tokugawa called the youthful retainer before him and gave him his orders. He was to race as quickly as possible to his home in Yagyumura to convince his father to persuade the local warrior families to side with Tokugawa in the coming war. With the aid of these backwoods lords, he planned to force Ishida's armies into a disadvantageous position and win the conclusive engagement.

Over lonely mountain passes and through damp forests of pine and scented cryptomeria, the retainer galloped his horse, fully aware that his was a mission of crucial importance. In retrospect, he probably had no idea how important, for in the humid summer of 1600 it might very well be said that the entire future of Japan rested on the ride of the solitary Tokugawa retainer, the son of Muneyoshi, Yagyu Munenori.

Yagyu Tajima no kami Munenori was born the youngest of eleven children in 1571 in Yagyumura, the village named after his family. With four older brothers, it is surprising that Munenori got any attention at all from his father. Yet the fates of war that kept Muneyoshi almost constantly in his armor during the last years of the sixteenth century had been varied. In the same year Munenori was born, his father and eldest brother Yoshikatsu were involved in a fierce battle at Tatsuichi. During the conflict, Yoshikatsu was wounded and permanently crippled. As the firstborn son, and a carefully groomed expert bugeisha, it was Yoshikatsu who would inherit both the control of the Yagyu clan and its holdings in Nara, and the headmastery of the Shinkage school. After his wounding, however, that inheritance was in doubt. As a ryu rapidly emerging as among the most respected in the land, Muneyoshi had to be most prudent as to who would represent it. Yoshikatsu would succeed his father as head of the family, but the head of the Shinkage ryu, Muneyoshi decided, would be granted to another. The next two Yagyu sons in line for the title proved capable swordsmen while still in their teens, but early in life both had shown a preference for the special discipline and austerity of the life of a Buddhist priest, and it was this way they elected to pursue rather than the dangerous path of the bugeisha. Another son, Munetoshi, was dutiful in his kenjutsu training, but Muneyoshi concluded that he had no special flair for swordsmanship, none of the natural talent that could drive him to further preserve and refine the ryu in his own time. He had not, as Nobutsuna perceived in Muneyoshi himself, the spirit of genius that stopped at nothing less than perfection. Therefore, though it ran contrary to all tradition, the head of the Shinkage ryu undertook to train his youngest son in the techniques of the New Shadow style, with the intention of naming him as its eventual master.

According to tales told around old Yagyumura, Munenori was a most adept pupil with a bursting enthusiasm for learning swordcraft. One story about him concerns an exercise he created on his own to improve his footwork and timing. Taking several lengths of twine, he tied small stones to each and then fixed the other to the overhanging branches of a copse of cedars near the Koyagyu mansion. Tugging on the suspended stones set the branches bouncing and when all of them were in motion, Munenori took a stance in their midst, slashing and cutting with his bokken, trying to touch as many of the moving stones as possible without losing his balance or control.

Another story of Munenori's childhood tells of his determination to harden himself for the physical rigors demanded of the kenjutsu master. It occurred in the wintertime, when Yagyumura was knee-deep in mountain snow and most of the villagers stayed huddled inside around their *kotatsu*, the fireplace pits that were a popular place in the otherwise unheated Japanese home. Munenori, though, regarded the snow as a convenient training aid. Naked except for his *fundoshi* loincloth, he would plow through the drifts, sword swinging madly, using the mass of the snow as a means of strengthening his legs. Under such harshly self-imposed conditions, the Yagyu youth would practice until his thighs and calves turned blue from the cold, retreating to a servant masseur's ministrations only when he could barely continue to walk.

In young Munenori's day, as it had been for Muneyoshi and Nobutsuna, rugged and unrelenting training was considered a normal part of the education of a bugeisha. In addition to his private practice, Munenori also took lessons daily in his father's dojo at Koyagyu, in kenjutsu as well as in the arts of the spear and naginata. Muneyoshi also tutored his child in what he believed to be his own specialty, the techniques of *kumi-uchi*, unarmed forms of grappling from which the art of *jujutsu* later evolved.

The samurai and bugeisha were rarely without their weapons, so they had little use for empty hand methods of fighting. But occasionally a sword or spear would be broken in combat, leaving the samurai unarmed, and the bugeisha might be attacked at an unexpected moment and then both would be forced to resort to the skills of kumi-uchi.

In comparison to the modern judo that descended from it, kumi-uchi was vicious, with little regard for the niceties of fair play. Many of the throws or immobilizing pins of the weaponless fighting depended upon applying leverage against an opponent's joints or points of balance. The samurai's treasured, carefully coiffured topknot (*chomage*) was a convenient handle that could be grabbed and twisted to control an opponent. Some exponents studied the construction of the warrior's armor, devising ways to grip and pull on a bushi's helmet or his armguards to inflict injury. They combined their grappling with *tantojutsu*, the use of a short dagger, training to penetrate weak spots in the armor with the sharp blade. Kicks and edge of the hand blows against vulnerable areas were also included in kumi-uchi, as were strangling techniques and joint locks that snapped bones and tendons with split second efficiency.

The kumi-uchi practiced by members of the Shinkage ryu was largely the creation of Muneyoshi, who polished the lessons he had learned in the Tomita ryu dojo of his first master during his wartime experience. When he applied to the throws, locks, and strikes of kumi-uchi the same principles he had been taught in kenjutsu by Nobutsuna, he initiated the development of a lethal system of self-defense for the unarmed bugeisha that became known in the teaching of the Shinkage school as *muto,* or "without sword."

The muto kumi-uchi of the Shinkage ryu served its most useful purpose in 1594, when Tokugawa Ieyasu invited Muneyoshi along with his twenty-four-year-old son Munenori, to demonstrate his art at the Tokugawa mansion in Kyoto. Tokugawa, always the farsighted strategist, was already plotting and planning for the day when Hideyoshi would be dead and the reins of Japan's government would be up for grabs. It's entirely possible, in fact, that he invited the Yagyu swordsmen to his home and courted their favor with the future in mind, hoping that they would be a useful aid in a contest for power in that part of the country. If so, however, this reason must have soon become a matter of secondary importance to Tokugawa that evening in his garden, for at the culmination of the demonstration he found himself, sword in hand, facing the legendary master Muneyoshi.

Their encounter came as a result of a question Tokugawa asked of the Shinkage ryu headmaster. On sections of clean straw tatami matting laid on the ground in front of the dais where the daimyo and his chief retainers sat, Muneyoshi and Munenori had already performed a selection of the distinctive kata of the Shinkage school. All of the audience were hardened warriors, all had trained most of their lives in the bujutsu, and all of them were difficult to impress. Even so, the Tokugawa retainers leaned forward as the demonstration continued, eyes narrowing in pleasure and concentration as, swords flashing, father and son leaped at one another, pirouetting, charging, and evading with flawless rhythm and control.

The samurai of the Tokugawa clan were open in their admiration, but their leader, typical of a man of his insight, believed he had seen more than just an excellent example of swordsmanship. Watching the performance, he had gotten the impression that the elder Yagyu was able to foresee almost magically the direction and force of his son's attacks and to counter them even as they were begun. He posed a question to Muneyoshi that he hoped would test his suspicions.

"Yagyu Sensei!" Even in ordinary conversation, the daimyo's voice rang with the authority of a commander's. "As you've said, your style of fencing depends upon correctly timed body movement, so an opponent's sword is countered with a counterattack of your own." Muneyoshi nodded. "But how would an unarmed fencer of the Shinkage ryu fare against a swordsman?"

Muneyoshi regarded Tokugawa with cold calculation. Many of his fellow lords back in the mountains of the Kinki region were confident that the diminutive, permanently scowling general Tokugawa was on the verge of launching himself into a glorious future and it would be no minor advantage for the Yagyu family to be connected to him. Muneyoshi was also a shrewd man, as quick-witted as his host, and he was guessing that if the Shinkage ryu was ever to distinguish itself from the scores of other bujutsu schools vying for attention, the moment had come. He bowed until his forehead touched the matting.

"If your lordship will assist me, I will show him."

The bold reply was a gamble that worked. Tokugawa Ieyasu rose, stepped down from the dais, and selected a bokken from the rack of weapons placed nearby for the demonstration. Clad in a silk hakama and *kamishimo* (a formal vest with stiff, winglike shoulders) that he wore over his kimono, he assumed a fighting posture against the simply dressed Yagyu master who, for all his skill, was, nevertheless, in the eyes of the Tokugawa nobles, merely a minor lord from a backwater hamlet.

Of all the spectators, only young Munenori was sure of the outcome of the "duel." He had seen his father in action too many times at the Koyagyu dojo; he knew too well the strength of the Shinkage ryu's muto, to doubt. Muneyoshi's empty-handed methods were not so much a matter of technique as they were a total mastery of timing, employed when an enemy created an opening in an attack, an incalculably brief instant when his mind was separated from his body. Since the muto required movement at that moment, exposing oneself to a katana that was perhaps already in motion, reactions had to be faultless, evading the attack and seizing the enemy's sword at its hilt or, almost unbelievably to those watching, catching its blade between the palms of the hands, disarming the swordsman with a wrenching throw that ended the fight conclusively. The Shinkage muto techniques allowed not a hairsbreadth of hesitation. The second at which they were executed had to be so precise that one of the first teachings of the ryu was this: "The difference between the living and the dying is in the timing."

Before Muneyoshi's calm gaze, Tokugawa advanced, a well-muscled and utterly fearless samurai approaching a bugeisha twenty years his senior, who stood expressionless, his empty hands extending outward at the level of his waist.

Tokugawa struck in a blur. His hips snapped down, sinking his body along with the blow that seemed to have connected, but Muneyoshi was not under the wooden blade. He pivoted fractionally, reversed, and shot out his arm, hurling Tokugawa backward, the bokken flying with equal force in the opposite direction. Everyone in the garden froze. The Tokugawa officers were motionless on the platform, awed. Munenori, on the other edge of the tatami, was still. Between him and the dais, sprawled on the matting, Lord Tokugawa eyed the fencing master who stood unruffled above him. At last, he nodded solemnly.

"Suki desu!" he said simply. "I like it."

On the spot Muneyoshi was requested to become the private fencing instructor for Tokugawa and his family. For any swordsman, the position was the finest occupation imaginable. With the position came a guarantee of advancement to the samurai rank of *hatamoto* (one of the chief retainers of a major daimyo), a healthy stipend insuring wealth for generations to come, and considerable influence in political and social circles. Though Muneyoshi was honored by the offer, he declined, suggesting politely instead that his son might be suitable for the job. Once again, Tokugawa had reason to be impressed with the wisdom of the Shinkage ryu headmaster. By nominating his son, he had assured Munenori's future in the perilous days he suspected were ahead for Japan. Already in his mid-sixties, Muneyoshi would soon be retiring from teaching swordsmanship, but by placing Munenori so closely to the Tokugawa clan, he could be confident that the fortunes of the house of Yagyu would remain intact.

Munenori was given the task of training Ieyasu and the rest of the Tokugawa family in kenjutsu. In return, Tokugawa gratefully presented Muneyoshi with a written pledge that he would abide by the rules of the Shinkage ryu and that he would always provide for the needs of members of the Yagyu family.

And so from such a past Yagyu Munenori came to be the teacher and retainer of Tokugawa Ieyasu. It was in that way that, in the summer of 1600, he came to be riding over the Tokkaido highway, racing for Yagyumura to a conference with his father that would aid his lord in winning the battle for the title of shogun.

Contrary to the Chinese saying that "in the third generation comes destruction," Munenori was of a character equally as strong as his father's and grandfather's. In covert meetings, he and Muneyoshi convinced the lords of the Kinki district to side themselves with Tokugawa, dispatching a group of them immediately to assist the samurai who were guarding Fushimi Castle against Mitsunari Ishida. No complete records remain of these secret dealings conducted by the Yagyu, but the assistance rendered by them to Tokugawa in his bid for the shogunate is quite clear.

Also lost to history is Munenori's private rendezvous with his brother Munetoshi, though it must have been a successful reunion, as incidents over the following month proved, also bettering Tokugawa's chances for victory. Munetoshi, the Yagyu son who had been judged by his father to be of incapable ambition to head the ryu had, in the meantime, become a highly ranked advisor to Kobayakawa Hideaki, an ally of Ishida's.

With all the players drawing together on the stage, events progressed rapidly, though not exactly according to the plans of Ishida and his pro-Toyotomi supporters. The pincer designed to snare Tokugawa was spoiled when Fushimi Castle failed to capitulate. Augmented by Kinki samurai and guerrilla warfare experts called *shinobi-nin*, or *ninja*, Tokugawa's contingent at the castle held Ishida off day after day. When he finally overran the fortress and started a forced advance to get his half of the pincer in place, it was too late. Losing confidence, Uyesugi Kagekatsu, the other half of the trap, held his troops back, waiting to see what would happen before committing himself. Ishida, deprived of the pincer, shifted his army to the mouth of a picturesque, U-shaped valley known by the local name of Sekigahara, where he was soon joined by his allies, a combined force totalling ninety thousand men. Though he was still outnumbered by Tokugawa's one hundred thousand samurai, his move was ingenious. When Tokugawa attacked, he would be led into the valley and outflanked, to be slaughtered by Ishida's troops surging in from both sides.

The rains began on the night of September 14. With a rumble, the sky dissolved and leaked a steady downpour. In their tents, samurai checked the fittings of their equipment and wondered about the mud that would make fighting even more exhausting. Lower ranked ashigaru (foot soldiers), with nothing to protect them from the showers but their lances, huddled miserably, trying to decide if battle could be worse than shivering in the cold wetness.

By morning, the rain had lessened to a gray drizzle, almost invisible in a clammy fog that thickened at dawn, blurring the outlines of men only yards away and losing the valley to sight entirely. With their soaking armor creaking, Tokugawa's troops set out toward Sekigahara along a road they hoped would lead them into the middle of the wide plain where, according to scouts, Ishida was supposed to be. In the white blindness, though, no one could be sure of anything, except that they were following the vague shapes of their comrades in front of them.

Sekigahara is sometimes described in the history books as the "Gettysburg of Japan." For the participants, it was a terrifying, confusing mess. The battle started when Ishida and Tokugawa samurai stumbled across each other in the fog. Literally scores of generals were directing their men and, even in the best of conditions, it was inevitable that things would have gone awry. As it was, units of the same army found themselves advancing upon one another, others were lost completely, and some, restrained by leaders like Kagekatsu who wavered, never got into the action at all. Ranks of musketeers cursed the dampness that fouled the firing mechanisms of their clumsy guns. Spearmen and swordsmen mingled in deadly intercourse, all of them scrambling for position on a field that was chopped to gummy slime under the hooves of cavalry mounts. Adding to the melee was the stupefying noise of shouted orders, the screams of the wounded, and the roar of exploding matchlocks—all amplified and distorted by the fog. That was Sekigahara on the morning of September 15, 1600.

In spite of the gigantic confusion, it still looked as if Ishida would prevail as the battle progressed. Tokugawa had funneled his samurai into the opening of the valley in a full charge after the enemy and Ishida played his role as the bait, retreating slowly to pull Tokugawa in. Ishida was waiting for his ally Kobayakawa Hideaki to rush down from the hills to smash Tokugawa, when once again the efforts of the pro-Toyotomi regents were thwarted.

Through Munenori's coaxing, his brother Munetoshi had persuaded his lord to switch sides at the crucial moment. Instead of attacking Tokugawa, Kobayakawa joined him and together they dashed at Ishida's headquarters. The battle in the valley ended with an awful swiftness. By the day's dusk Ishida was dead, his Toyotomi allies scattered in headlong flight and demoralized. The triumph at Sekigahara was the final step in Tokugawa's scheme for dominance, and before the bodies had even been removed from the valley, there was talk that he would be appointed by the emperor as Seii Taishogun, the Great Barbarian Quelling General, the military ruler of Japan.

Tokugawa Ieyasu's clever plotting and his good fortune were always a mark of his victories. It was his trust in his Yagyu retainer and his study of the Shinkage ryu's philosophy, though, that won him the battle of Sekigahara. In that terrible valley of death, the difference between the living and the dying had indeed been in the timing.

Munenori received the news of the battle at Koyagyu. The sturdy *amado* screens were slid back to reveal the groves of maple that surrounded the family home, and while an unseasonable breeze fluttered their leaves in a soft, leathery applause, he sat alone in deep contemplation of what Tokugawa's victory meant for the future of the ryu of which he would soon be headmaster. He had much to prepare for. Sekigahara marked the beginning of a 270-year era of unification under Tokugawa rule for Japan. For Yagyu Munenori and the Shinkage ryu, it was the beginning of an ascendancy to fame unequalled in the annals of Japanese swordsmanship.

9.
Iai, Cutting at Raindrops

As with other tools crafted to make wars, a cult has grown up around the katana, the long sword of the samurai. Tales are told, as they have been for centuries, of swords that leaped from their scabbards of their own volition to save their owners in times of danger; of weapons with blades so sharp they could slice through three or four hapless bodies stacked atop one another at execution grounds *tameshigiri*, "tests of cutting"; of swords that, by their very excellence, conferred upon the men who possessed them either a greatness of character or a vicious madness. Even if these stories and legends are discounted, the lengthy history and intricate lore of the katana give to it a certain air of awesome mystery, heightened by its terrible beauty and the undeniable fact that the sword forged by Japanese smiths during the feudal age eventually reached a degree of perfection unmatched in any weapon before or since.

The Japanese sword originated its distinctive qualities during the Heian era (794-1190). Up until that time, the bladed arms of the early bushi were long and straight, modeled after prototypes from neighboring China. Fighting principally from horseback, the bushi had little problem with such a weapon, but once engaged in individual duels on the ground, he often found that the long sword was unwieldly and easily broken. A story has it that a Heian swordsmith stood among a crowd of villagers who were gathered to watch their lord and his army return home from a distant battle. As the ranks came marching past, it was obvious by their shattered and bent swords that they had met with defeat. The swordsmith was so ashamed of his inferior work that he couldn't meet the eyes of his lord when the daimyo rode by. He retreated to a solitary mountain hermitage for more than a year, praying to Shinto deities, purifying himself by constant exposure to nature's elements, living like the ascetic followers of Shugendo (the esoteric offshoot of Shingon Buddhism). At the end of his self-imposed exile, the story goes, the smith was granted by the gods the secrets of swordsmithery.

By the beginning of the Kamakura period (1185-1333), the effects of the divinely inspired smith's work were reflected in swords throughout Japan. The weapon had kept its long handle, allowing a firm, two-handed grip, but its cutting edge was shortened and the blade was given a curvature that strengthened it and lent to it a better stability for thrusting.

The most important change the sword underwent, however, was in the manner of its construction. Swordsmiths experimenting with a number of different metallurgical processes came up with a method of refining iron into a steel that was beyond anything known anywhere else in the world. Raw iron was heated amidst ritual prayer and the invocation of the gods. Then the smith and his assistants rhythmically pounded the bar of metal until it was flattened out, glowing orange in the darkened forge, to be folded over and the treatment begun again. After being repeatedly folded, hammered flat, and folded once more, the elements within the iron were fused into a strip of steel that possessed remarkable durability. At this stage of the forging a less meticulous craftsman might well have been content with his product. The finest smiths, though, sought not only to make a durable sword, but to make a sword that would hold and maintain a perfect sharpness. To temper this kind of edge, the smith coated the ridge and flat surface of the blade with various concoctions; their compounds were always a matter of deep secret although usually made principally of wet clay with other ingredients added to control the baking of the steel. When the katana had been fired until its edge was white hot, it was plunged into water. From the sputtering steam and the exploding clay emerged the bushi's ideal weapon: a sword with a ridge and spine malleable enough to endure in an almost indestructible manner and an edge so keen that when stuck into a brook, a leaf carried against it by the stream's gentle current would be sliced in two.

The first time I held a katana, four hundred years old and forged by the master Tsunemitsu, my thoughts were not of ancient stories or supernatural powers, but of the simple, undecorated utility of the thing. Whatever may be said of the sword's beauty and grace, those are matters of interest mainly to the collector or the swordsmith himself. For the swordsman, the bugeisha, the quality of a sword is almost entirely a matter of practicality. It is meant for cutting, and if there is to be anything realized beyond that, it is something that can only come after thousands upon thousands of hours of cutting, so naturally the bugeisha appreciated and respected a sword that does that well.

The katana Kotaro Sensei handed me had an exquisite temper-line that reminded me of a horizon of bright, undulating clouds. On its guard was a tiny tableau of crows circling in flight (*tomoe karasu*), illustrating a combat strategy of the Yagyu Shinkage school. Yet what Sensei pointed out to me was the narrow, angled tip of the sword, designed to penetrate an opponent's body quickly. He demonstrated its balance, a weapon built for the fastest movement possible. He noted the grooved blood gutters that ran down both sides of the blade, making it less susceptible to breakage during a strong cut; the groove also channels an enemy's blood off the steel so that it won't soil the sword. Sensei spoke brusquely, dealing matter of factly with the business of dispatching a human being most violently. And while my teacher was the gentlest of

103

men, he made it clear that the art of drawing a sword, *iaijutsu*, was a matter of considerable seriousness.

In the Yagyu Shinkage ryu, iaijutsu is known by one of its many alternative names, *battojutsu, batto* being a term signifying a draw and strike in an initial movement with the sword. Its methods are comprised of the *saya no uchi batto gohon*, the five basic techniques of drawing and cutting, although there are a larger number of variations stemming from these fundamentals. Before I could practice any of them, however, I had to start at the beginning again.

The philosophical and strategic mentality behind iaijutsu is central to the education of the bugeisha, something made simpler to understand through the connotation behind the word "*iai.*" The "i" (pronounced as "e") refers to a dynamic carriage of one's body when in a state of readiness. The *kamae*, or stances, Sensei and I took during kata with the bokken are examples of i, as are the times at judo training when students come together in *kumi kata* to grip one another's lapels and sleeves before commencing a judo match. The character "ai" means a centering of the spirit, or the ki. In a broader sense, the ai of iaijutsu refers to the individual's ability to center himself within the framework of his family, his society, his country, and eventually, within the world and the universe. So together, iai calls to mind a positioning of the swordsman's body and spirit that results in and demonstrates his continuity with the environment around him.

Since the sword-drawing art was developed to protect the bugeisha when he was attacked unexpectedly, it was performed from his everyday postures: standing, sitting, even lying down. I was introduced to training in it by learning to squat in *iaigoshi*, a special variation of seiza that allowed for rapid and unrestricted movement from a seated position. Iaigoshi requires the swordsman to kneel, weight resting on his left leg, his right bent and pointing forward. (If a sprinter in his blocks were to squat down lower, he would end up in something similar to iaigoshi.) The whole posture is a kind of crouch that stretched my toes in the first few weeks I practiced it, a unique discomfort that, Sensei assured me, had been withstood by generations of bugeisha. He showed me how to use iaigoshi to spring up quickly. By dropping my forward knee, lifting the other, and pivoting, I could move along the floor, and never raise myself at all, a useful ability for the bugeisha who lived in a culture where everyone sat on the floors. Iaigoshi was also used practically by the samurai when he scouted an enemy's position and wanted to remain concealed close to the ground.

When I could walk along the dojo floor on my knees as swiftly as Sensei could move beside me standing up, he judged me ready to go on to the Yagyu battojutsu's next posture, *tachi-iai*. To the un-initiated, the swordsman in tachi-iai is merely standing erect. Fol-lowing Sensei's instruction, though, revealed a number of distinc-tions. He carefully adjusted my stance so my weight rested on the balls of my feet, for greater mobility. Head held back even with my shoulder, buttocks tightened, eyes forward, the posture disclosed the intent of tachi-iai: to become the essence of zanshin, the alert, always ready state of mind necessary to excel in the world of the classical martial arts.

Once I was accustomed to crouching and moving in iaigoshi, Kotaro Sensei showed me the etiquette of handling the sheathed katana. When not actually wearing it, I carried it at my side, thumb wrapped over the *tsuba*, or guard, so that even if I leaned over and tilted the scabbard the sword wouldn't come sliding out acciden-tally. If I sat in seiza, I kept the sword on the floor on my left side, near my knee, ready to be drawn. Before training, I knelt by the kamiza shrine in the dojo and placed the katana in front of me, bowing formally to it and symbolizing *kenshin ittai*, the sword and mind becoming one. In wearing the katana in its scabbard, or *saya*, for practice, I wedged it into the wrappings of my obi at the proper angle along my left hip. I always kept my left hand on the saya, gripping it a handspan from the hilt, in preparation for *nukitsuke*, the draw.

While I would never have qualified as a teenage daredevil, I certainly took my share of risks during those years. I spent many weekends at the end of a rope, scrambling up the faces of crumbly limestone cliffs with mountaineering friends in the Ozark hills. I played right wing on a Rugby team, the only high school player in a collegiate league filled with university players twice my size. And my seniors at judo seemed to have an inexhaustible supply of training that threatened life and limb. But unleashing a yard-long, wickedly sharp sword out of a scabbard inches from my belly, slashing with it, and then sliding it back into its sheath, again only a finger's distance from my abdomen, was one of the most frightening things I had ever done. It was worse by far than the time my best friend and I went canoeing on a flooded river and nearly drowned. Worse even than the stormy night a girlfriend and I explored a lonely country cemetery and ended up sheltering ourselves from an unearthly onslaught of lightning and rain in a deserted and equally spooky old church, complete with creaking floorboards. I'd start getting nervous about iaijutsu practice early in the day, usually during Earth Science. It was the only distraction that could occupy more of my attention than Linda Smith's legs, stretched out two rows in front of me. Teachers who saw me walking to classes with a fretful look about me probably concluded I was worried about acne, or a relationship with a girl like Linda Smith. It's a safe bet they never suspected I was really wondering how many stitches it would take to close the gash opened by a carelessly handled samurai katana.

Though I never had a serious accident at Sensei's dojo, once, in returning the blade to its scabbard I ran the point over my finger and nicked it, scaring me so badly that I nearly dropped the sword. Sensei was endlessly patient, however, and he demonstrated for me the minor, almost unnoticeable techniques that can reduce the danger of iaijutsu somewhat. He showed me how to push with my left thumb and forefinger against the sword's guard, just before the nukitsuke, clearing the stopperlike *habaki*, the metal collar separating hilt and blade, from the saya. In place, the habaki provides enough friction to keep the sword in its sheath, and when it is pushed out, it permits the katana to be drawn smoothly, without jerking it free of the scabbard. Likewise, at the resheathing of the katana, the left hand moves the saya forward a bit, helping to ease the sword back into place. This finesse with the left hand Sensei referred to as *monouchi no kiri*, or "cutting at the scabbard mouth," and he insisted I practice it until every facet became natural.

Another technique used to protect the swordsman in iaijutsu comes just before he resheathes his katana in the final movement, called *noto*. Since he must maintain zanshin, the bugeisha cannot be looking down at his side to make sure the sword is fitted into the mouth of his scabbard. The action must be done by feel, without the aid of sight to guide it. To facilitate this, the iaijutsu exponent is trained to bring his sword up even with the scabbard, holding it horizontally across his body. Then, cupping the fingers of his left hand over the opening of the scabbard and beginning at the tsuba, he draws the back of the blade through their pinching grip. Reaching the end of the katana and fitting it into the saya, he reverses the motion, sliding the sword into its sheath in a single, fluid motion that looks almost magical.

The most vital part of iaijutsu is in the *kime*, the focusing of the sword's strike which occurs simultaneously with its unsheathing. Pulling a katana from its saya with speed is largely a mechanical act, one that I learned in a relatively short time. (It's the same thing most of the actors in Japanese samurai movies are taught to do to make their choreographed fight scenes more dramatic.) The ultimate aim of the bugeisha's sword drawing art, though, is to unsheathe the blade with all possible speed and then to strike, hard, decisively, and without a pause in the acceleration of the draw. This sort of lethal whipping action, a combination of the nukitsuke and the focus of the blow, is called *kisagake* in the Yagyu Shinkage ryu. It is the very essence of the art, the mark of the *kenshi*, or master swordsman. According to the principles of the ryu, Sensei explained, this instantaneous draw and cut was likened to the sound and spark of flint striking steel. Between the two, there could be no discernible space, no room for an opponent to escape.

Draw, cut, and resheathe. Draw, turn, and cut behind. Draw, parry, and thrust. My schoolbooks were stacked in a corner of the dojo while I practiced to make my iai with the swiftness of the sound and the spark. Watching over my efforts, Kotaro Sensei habitually employed a favorite method of his for making a point—just lightly he would kick or swing the flat ridge of a bokken against my hips or under my arms. During the first months of my training in the bujutsu, I had thought his strikes, like those to my legs, were a kind of harsh encouragement, urging me on. When I began to study with a real sword, however, he seemed to concentrate on the blows and frequently he would shout, "Settsuku, squeeze, squeeze, settsuku."

"What's settsuku, Sensei?" I finally asked, mystified by a word I couldn't find in any Japanese-English dictionary.

"Means 'all together,' everything same time."

I assumed this to mean I wasn't going fast enough, and I increased my speed, pulling the katana out and slashing as quickly as I could. But the strikes continued, as did the exhortation to "settsuku." The breakdown in communication continued painfully until I went to visit Dr. Young, a professor of Japanese history at the university. His Japanese wife and his knowledge of the language and customs of Japan had been helpful to me before.

"Dr. Young," I ran up to him outside his office in the history department. "What the hell is settsuku?"

"Connection," he answered.

"Connection?" I asked Sensei the next day after he had tapped at my ribs again.

"Ah, yes, yes. Connection. Everything connected." He took the sword and showed me what he meant. He cut the air in front of him and while his attack was powerful, it lacked something. Then he struck once more and this time it was as if he was really cutting the air itself—it made that kind of noise. Watching it, I had no doubts that the katana in his hands would have gone through an opponent as efficiently as it sliced through the empty space.

"Don't just cut with arms. Strike with whole body." Again he slashed vertically, yet instead of gripping the katana's hilt firmly with both hands as he had taught me, he held it only with the thumb and forefinger of each hand. I was wide-eyed in amazement when he struck as forcefully as before, controlling the sword with four fingertips. What Sensei was trying to do with his feat—the reason behind all that shouting and slapping and kicking—was make me realize that just the strength of my arms or hands couldn't do that much. They had to be combined with the connected power of the shoulders, hips, and legs; all parts of the body working together in a single, unified force so that the katana became an extension of it. That is settsuku.

The difference between an attack that has settsuku and one that lacks settsuku can be seen when comparing the punch of a karate expert with that of a boxer's. The boxer is conditioned to use his arms in swinging hooks and jabs, so he punches at weighted bags and does all sorts of exercises to make his arms as muscular as possible. The karateman, in contrast, is encouraged to strike from his hips, so he concentrates on developing his whole body to work as a unit. As a result, the boxer's punch stuns—the karateka's shatters and kills.

I grew much better at connecting my body to the sword once my teacher introduced me to tameshigiri, or test cutting, which is for the katana what striking against the tire had been for my bokken training. In the old days, tameshigiri was, well, unusual. It is explained in the journals of the sixteenth century bushi Yamamoto Tsunetomo.

"Yamamoto Kichizaemon was ordered by his father to cut down a dog at the age of five, and at the age of fifteen he was made to execute a criminal. Everyone, by the time they were fourteen or fifteen, was ordered to do a beheading without fail. When Lord Katsushige was young, he was ordered by Lord Naoshige to practice killing with a sword. It is said that at the time he was made to cut down more than ten men successively."

"Tameshigiri" is composed of two words, *tameshi* (spirit) and *giri* or *kiri* (to cut), and in the gruesome training methods of the days Yamamoto was writing about, it must surely have been a test of one's spirit at cutting. Often the bodies of executed criminals were stacked on a specially constructed mound for the purpose of seeing how many could be cleaved with a single stroke of the sword. Other times a corpse was strung up on a frame and the swordsman practiced his techniques according to detailed patterns of cutting—labeled with names like "priest's robe cut," "waterwheel strike," and "stone stroke"—that were graded with varying degrees of difficulty. It's still common for sword collectors to come across antique blades that passed those trials, with inscriptions on the tangs ascertaining to the cutting performance of the weapon in execution ground tameshigiri.

The bujutsu have not changed all that much since their feudal beginnings, it's true, but understandably tameshigiri has been toned down a little. I asked Sensei about the old ways.

"Yes," he sighed. "Too hard to get bodies now. Also, it looks bad in the yard. Too messy."

Sensei was kidding, but he had a sword that had been used by his teacher's teacher that was engraved on the tang with the words "Brought down cleanly—three men," followed by the date of the testing, 1828; not that long ago.

For tameshigiri now, sheaves of straw are dampened and then twisted or woven into different thicknesses. These can be stacked or propped upright and the swordsman has a chance to practice his cutting technique against a resistant material. Because it's wet, the straw is quite tough, not easily cut through, and if the stroke is not quick and delivered with sufficient force, the swordsman is likely to end up with a faceful of flying straw as his target disintegrates halfway through his cut. I hacked and chopped my way through several bales of the stuff, reducing four-foot sheaves the thickness of my leg to satisfying piles of fodder and fantasizing all kinds of battles and duels in the process. I cut down thousands of foes and exercised a lot of adolescent energy against that straw, which might well be one of the benefits of tameshigiri.

I dueled with my fantasy enemies under the pines in Sensei's back yard. One day he was in the dojo, crouched in iaigoshi before a length of wrapped straw that was held off the floor, stretched across a wooden platform that resembled a short legged bench turned upside down. Sensei held his katana poised above his head for a second, then struck, whacking through the straw except for a few strands that held the piece together when both ends fell. The result was a little mountain peak of straw under his blade. Sensei told me to sweep the straw out and after I had done it and begun my own practice, he came back and explained to me the purpose of his tameshigiri. Without the straw target, he put me in the same position, corrected my posture, and instructed me in how to bring the katana down along an imaginary line drawn parallel to my big toe, stopping the stroke and pulling the sword back up abruptly.

"This is the cut for the *kaishaku*," he said, and I understood then why the strike was so short and retracted rather than carried through. When he wanted to make an ultimate demonstration of his sincerity, to prove a point, or when he was ordered to do so by his superiors for some error or crime, the bushi committed suicide by *seppuku*, plunging a short sword into the left side of his abdomen, drawing it across his belly, and exposing literally what he considered to be the very repository of his soul. Seppuku began when a chief retainer of the Minamoto clan was defeated while defending his castle from a besieging army. In cold frustration at his loss, the retainer climbed a castle tower and before the eyes of his astonished enemies, he disemboweled himself, tossing a handful of his own intestines onto the attackers below and then dying by severing his spinal cord.

As disembowelment became the accepted form of suicide for the samurai, the Minamoto retainer's spontaneous act grew into a ritual, its every aspect formalized. Dressed in white, the Buddhist color signifying death, the warrior seated himself in seiza and took up a sword from a tray beside him. If his immolation was to take place in front of his peers, he sometimes made a short speech, announcing the reasons for his actions. Tucking his sleeves under his knees to keep himself from writhing in an unseemly manner during his dying throes, the bushi ended his life with the same steel that might well have saved it many times before.

Not every samurai possessed the almost superhuman strength of the Minamoto retainer who sliced through his spine to finish his suffering; disembowelment was a long and horrible way to die. For that reason, the kaishaku came to be. Ironically chosen from among the condemned man's closest friends was a swordsman who knelt beside him at the moment of death, katana ready. The kaishaku's role was to wait and watch, judging at what instant the pain became too great for the man dying before him to withstand, and then he struck, aiming his blow along the neck's hairline, cutting surely to take off the head and put an end to the agony of seppuku. Yet it would not do for the samurai's head to go rolling away like a chunk of wood under the chopper's axe. The kaishaku's job was to prevent that, to stop his cut just at the point where a bit of skin remained to connect the head with the neck. This skill, called *daki-kubi*, required considerable ability and was the proof of a competent kaishaku.

In 1970, while I was training with my sensei, we were surprised by the untimely death of the author Yukio Mishima who, in protest of recent social tendencies in Japan, committed a dramatic seppuku at the headquarters of the Japan Defence Forces. Mishima followed the proper ritual of seppuku, even to leaving a final poem to express his feelings, but his kaishaku, a young student without experience in swordsmanship, became unnerved. After the student made several hacking tries, a general of the Defense Forces who was present took the katana from him and performed the cut correctly.

The sad death of Mishima, who had been an expert in the modern forms of fencing and sword drawing, was a reminder that the ways of the warrior were not merely a memory, but a living thing that was carried on through those of us who still trained in them.

I kept the analogy of flint and steel in mind and worked daily to bring the sound and the spark closer. Then one December day Sensei took me out to the old garage beside the house on the quiet street. Used as a storage shed by the landlord, the garage had a musty sawdust floor and the smells of carpentry made me sneeze. The wide door was lifted open and in spite of winter's brittle cold, the sunlight poured through, warming us and the snow that had piled in the rusty gutter overhead. Sensei stood in the doorway, facing the steady drip, drip, drip of melting snow. He moved me back out of the way, then assumed tachi-iai. His sword was a silvery flicker in the sunlight, making a sucking sound as it came out and raked horizontally, then stopping with focus. There was no question that he had hit the droplet; he did it again and again, never missing.

112

"Now you try," he said, and I did. I tried to draw the katana quickly, I tried drawing it slowly—all in an effort to catch the timing. I used my hip to add momentum to the action. I drew with careful attention and in unthinking irritation and if ever I endangered a single drop of water, it was through absolutely no fault of my own. The last of the winter's crusty snow had melted away and the plump raindrops of summer were gurgling and dribbling from the leaky gutter before I began to hit them with any regularity.

From the icy drips of winter to the softly plunking beads of the spring rain, the rhythm of the drips was of its own making, following a natural sequence that could only be met and followed, never forced. It did not help to hurry up or try to slow down in concentration. Mastery of a thing comes at its own pace.

Gravesite of the Yagyu clan in Yagyu village, Nara Prefecture. Many of the Yagyu sword masters are buried here.

10.
The Swordsman and the Priest

On the cedar floorboards, wide and scrubbed so often that the grain showed as if it were sanded, droplets of perspiration stained in little flat puddles. The sharp features of Yagyu Munenori were bathed in it. He paused to rub his face and throat with a small checkered towel and stuffed it back into his training jacket.

"Never, never, allow your enemy to raise his head once you've begun an attack." He resumed his lecture to the select class that gathered in the late winter evening at the Yagyu dojo in Edo. All senior students of the ryu, the group included an aide to the province's governor as well as three of the shogun's private guard—all proud swordsmen of the most elite fencing school in the capital city, all students of the shogun's own instructor, Yagyu Munenori, son of Yagyu Muneyoshi.

The master of the dojo beckoned to one of them, who stepped up and bowed to him.   Teacher and pupil were both wielding fukuro shinai, the leather and cloth padded stick with which Hikida Bungoro had beaten Muneyoshi at the Hozoin Temple years before. (Adopting the shinai for certain kinds of two-man practice because it was safer than the bokken, Muneyoshi had passed its use in training on to his son. Munenori, in turn, employed it with the ryu's advanced practitioners to teach them the finer details of making a strong attack.) The student took a firm stance, easing his shinai forward from his waist, aiming its tip directly at Munenori's face in the ryu's *seigan kamae*. The posture was meant to intimidate, which it could easily do since the opponent's attention was naturally centered on the point of the sword that was looming threateningly close to his face.

Munenori, however, swept past his student's on guard position as if his shinai were a spindly tree branch, to be pushed away like a minor annoyance. With a snapping wrench of his wrists, he stroked his own shinai down, forcing the student to skip back to block the blow. Munenori glided forward, like a malevolent wind rushing across the floor. He followed up his initial attack with another, aimed at the midsection. Again the disciple parried the strike, but he bent fractionally to meet its force, breaking his posture slightly in the process. Munenori was on him in an instant, unleashing a barrage of slashes and thrusts, his legs charging him like a battering ram run amok. His pupil, his defense totally broken, could do nothing but retreat, stumbling over himself in his effort to get away from the onslaught. Only when he was a foot's distance from the wall of the dojo and, by all indications, threatening to pass right through it in his eagerness to get out of Munenori's way, did the master of the Yagyu Shinkage style halt.

"Once his head is lowered, the connection between it and the hips is broken and so it is impossible for him to mount an offense." He bowed to his student. "You have but to continue your attack relentlessly to weaken him so he may be overcome."

Moments later, the class went to work on the day's lesson. Their hakama tucked up so that the hard muscles of their calves showed, they paired off and the dojo echoed with the leathery thuds as their shinai clashed, searching for the opening that would let them in to penetrate their training partner's defense. In the wet street outside the dojo, passersby hurried on their way in the lightly falling snow. The fire watcher made his rounds, shouting his warnings about untended fires in a lilting, singsong voice. A strolling vendor of grilled eel rubbed his hands and sniffed his wares. Each of them heard the sounds of the shinai smacking and the spirited shouts of the bugeisha and they regarded it with a sense of pride that their neighborhood was the home of the Edo Yagyu Shinkage ryu.

In 1604, Yagyu Muneyoshi took the epithet Sekishusai, a ritual name change that symbolized, as it did for many warriors who were followers of the Lord Buddha, that he had retired from temporal life. In his dojo at Koyagyu, he continued to practice kenjutsu and to teach a small retinue of disciples, but most of Muneyoshi's retirement years were taken with hunting expeditions in the Kinki highlands with his falcons and with sojourns to the mineral hot springs of the Arima spas in Settsu Province.

As he had planned, taking his place as the second headmaster of the Yagyu Shinkage school was his youngest son Munenori, and as the new leader of the ryu and with the Tokugawa shogun as his student, changes came in the life of the fencer from Yagyumura. To be near his daimyo, Munenori left his father's fief for Edo, having a fine samurai's home and a dojo built there. Edo, originally a swampy marshland in the lee of a shallow, funnel-shaped bay, became the Tokugawa capital after the establishment of Ieyasu's rule and, correspondingly, the rude little village there grew quickly, with the promise of developing into a sophisticated center of culture and commerce. Munenori's move from his mountain hamlet to the fashionable Edo district of Azabu was one he could well afford, for following the battle of Sekigahara his stipend was raised by the shogun to 3,000 *koku* of rice a year, the same given to the Tokugawa's chief hatamoto.*

---

* A *koku*, the standard measurement of rice and, by extension, of income, was equivalent to a little more than five bushels, about the amount an adult consumed in a year. Records show that the martial arts instructor to the Shogun who preceded Munenori was salaried at only 33 koku, an indication of the esteem with which Ieyasu held the Yagyu master.

Hatamoto were a daimyo's advisors and trusted right arms, chosen from among his most capable bushi.

The elevation of his position in Edo society also required Munenori to exchange his simple linen kimono and hakama for finer silk garments to conform to the cosmopolitan lifestyles of the capital. But no matter how expensive his wardrobe, Munenori's friends had continuing cause to tease him about his rustic footwear: for the Yagyu bugeisha could never accustom his feet to the lacquered, high platform *geta*, or clogs, that were preferred in the city, always tying on instead the rugged mountaineer's *zori* sandals of his native province.

The first two years of the Tokugawa reign were halcyon and prosperous for Japan, and for Munenori. At his new dojo in Edo, he supervised classes composed of Tokugawa samurai, affluent noblemen, and ambitious bugeisha eager to train with the shogun's sensei performed the basic sword exercises of the ryu. After these morning classes and a lunch of pickled vegetables and rice, his afternoons were taken with instructing Ieyasu privately. Even though the shogun was constantly harried with the myriad affairs of state, he remained a determined pupil of the Yagyu Shinkage ryu, accepting humbly both Munenori's criticism and the grueling workouts imposed upon him.

During one lesson, the habitually taciturn Munenori had particular reason to be harsh with his student; the shogun appeared preoccupied and kept stumbling over a fundamental movement. At length he apologized to his teacher, explaining that his inattention to kenjutsu that day was because of a worry about a daimyo from a distant province who had failed to deliver his quota of taxes. Ieyasu could not decide whether to punish the otherwise loyal lord or to give him another chance. He asked Munenori what he would do. Thinking it over, the sword master replied with a homily from his homeland.

"If wronged once, always forgive. Twice, forgive again, keeping in mind that even a repentant man can repeat a mistake." Only after two transgressions, Munenori advised, should punitive action be taken.

As the political leader of his country, Ieyasu was almost continually being given advice by well-meaning subordinates, yet in Munenori's homily was a simple wisdom. It brought to Ieyasu's mind his initial encounter with the Shinkage ryu, when he had been greatly impressed by Munenori's father, whose ability to read an opponent's intentions before they occurred had been nothing short of mystical. The Tokugawa shogun, his attention captured by Munenori's counsel, began to see the same qualities in Muneyoshi's son. Frequently, he and his sensei would finish his lessons with a stroll through the villa gardens where he would seek Munenori's opinions about this and that. Munenori knew nothing of government administration, of course, but he learned from Muneyoshi that intense training in the arts of taking a life could conversely lead to an understanding of making life better for others. Applying the principles of Yagyu Shinkage philosophy and strategy, Munenori was able to advise Ieyasu in an unusual, yet apparently quite successful way. In turn, Munenori gained deep insight into the ways martial art could benefit society.

In 1605, the pleasant succession of days spent fencing, teaching, and talking with his daimyo were abruptly disrupted for Munenori. Ieyasu announced that he was going into an early and unexpected retirement and that his successor would be his son Hidetada. The Tokugawa's still-bitter enemies were enraged. They demanded that the son of Toyotomi Hideyoshi, Hideyori, denied his rightful heritage by the defeat at Sekigahara, should be advanced to the position of the shogunate, and in retaliation, they promptly set about initiating all sorts of minor uprisings and rebellions among the peasant classes with the intention of discrediting Tokugawa rule. Eventually, the dissension festered by the Toyotomi stalwarts grew into warfare that Ieyasu and his son Hidetada could not ignore and once again a faithful retainer from the house of Yagyu put away his bokken and took up the real thing. Attired in the armor of his clan with the silver jingasa crest emblazoned on its chest, Munenori departed Edo and rode to Osaka to protect his daimyo.

The threat to the Tokugawa shogunate wasn't really serious and Hidetada proved to be as clever a strategist as his father, deflating much of the rebellion's energy with sincere promises of lower taxes and a relaxing of restrictive laws like those limiting travel. A rabid core of Toyotomi supporters, however, refused to be mollified, fortifying themselves behind the walls of Osaka Castle and vowing to die for their cause. It was during the campaign at Osaka that Munenori performed one of his most legendary feats, a display of swordsmanship that proved his mastery of the art and convinced bugeisha that his skill was probably without equal anywhere in Japan.

The incident took place during the Winter Battle of Osaka. The conflict was inconclusive, and the Tokugawa armies were forced to return for a final successful siege later the next summer. From a vantage point on a high bluff, Hidetada and an escort of his retainers, including Munenori, were watching the action on a flatland near the castle below. Their observation post was so far from the battle that they were having difficulty seeing it clearly. Yet even at that distance, Munenori was habitually careful not to relax zanshin.

His vigilance did not go to waste. Bursting from a thick copse of striped bamboo at the rear of the wooded bluff crashed a unit of enemy samurai, katana glinting in the sunlight. On a scouting mission, they had stumbled upon the Tokugawa group, recognized the just appointed shogun Hidetada, and were quick to make the most of the opportunity. Munenori moved before the youthful shogun and his staff recognized the danger. He tore his sword from its saya and raced at a right angle into the path of the charging samurai to cut off their advance. Like a crackling streak of lightning, his blade slashed at the group, catching one of its leaders in midstroke. He fell without a sound, blood spurting from a crooked gash that spilled open his abdomen. Munenori's katana had found exactly the right target, a weak connection in the warrior's armor between where the chest and loin protectors were joined.

The strategy of the Yagyu Shinkage style of kenjutsu taught a swordsman outnumbered in combat to take the offensive. This Munenori did, maneuvering steadily toward his left, keeping as many of the enemy in front of him as possible. He feinted, stalling an assailant who threatened with an overhead strike, then shifted and cut down another in a broad, horizontal sweep. Pivoting, his katana flashed once, twice, answered both times with the steely clang of parries, but at the third stroke, the defending samurai was off balance and he stepped directly into the blade that ended his life. A spearman at Munenori's side hesitated, then stabbed too late into the space where Munenori had been, dying before he even comprehended the error; Munenori's counterattack cut through the spearman's yari's shaft as well as his neck. By then Hidetada's officers had surrounded him, swords drawn, but most of the attacking samurai were dead or wounded, the rest in frantic retreat.

Scenes much like Munenori's fight at the Osaka bluff would one day become standard in samurai films. In actual combat, though, especially when a bugeisha was weighted down in bulky armor, attack and defense against multiple opponents was a rare and nearly impossible task. Munenori's victory under the worst of circumstances was a bloody confirmation of his prowess and of the worth of the Yagyu Shinkage style. Tales of the accomplishment did much to spread further the reputations of both.

Tokugawa Hidetada was never as enthusiastic about his kenjutsu training as Ieyasu had been. His concerns showed a singular devotion to solidifying his family's power so he could in time safely turn over the rule to Iemitsu, his son. Even so, he treated Munenori with the respect due a sensei. After saving Hidetada's life at the Winter Battle of Osaka, the master of the Yagyu Shinkage ryu was once again promoted in rank—he was now properly addressed as Yagyu Tajima no kami Munenori, the Lord Munenori of Yagyu— and given another increase in his stipend.

In contrast to Hidetada's lukewarm immersion into the bujutsu, his son Iemitsu, who assumed the title of shogun in 1624, was Munenori's most outstanding kenjutsu pupil of the Tokugawa regents. From the time he was a child, he practiced daily under Munenori's tutelage in the ryu, demonstrating a voracious appetite for learning the craft. To further stimulate Iemitsu's interest, Munenori saw to it that his eldest son, Yagyu Mitsuyoshi, was assigned as a page to Iemitsu. The two boys were nearly the same age and together they spent many hours practicing. As a boy, Mitsuyoshi was a little hellion, a child of incredible energy and enthusiasm who took a fiendish delight in the rough and tumble bujutsu sessions in his father's ryu. Placing him with another boy

121

like the equally impetuous Iemitsu served to encourage both of them in their headstrong ways. It also, to Munenori's satisfaction, assured his son's future, secure in the employment of the Tokugawa family, just as Munenori's father had succeeded in getting him the position as Ieyasu's teacher.

Few details exist relating the early years of Iemitsu or his lessons under Munenori. Little remains but a letter, brushed in a neat, boyish script by the teenaged and obviously intense student to his master. In it, Iemitsu complained that his sensei wasn't taking his education in the martial arts seriously enough. "How am I to advance myself in kenjutsu if you do not push me?" he wrote. "It is up to you to decide whether I will be a worthwhile practitioner of the Yagyu Shinkage ryu."

For a student to complain openly to his sensei was nothing short of shocking in an age when disciples of the bujutsu carefully paced themselves to walk several steps behind their masters out of a Confucian sense of respect and who never presumed to question them in any way. Normally, even if his pupil was the shogun himself, a good teacher's punishment for such impetuousness would have been brutal, followed almost certainly by expulsion from the ryu. In Iemitsu's case, though, Munenori said nothing at all. He continued to receive his brash disciple at the Edo dojo and their lessons went on as if the rude letter hadn't been written or read. Munenori happened to be working at the time with Iemitsu on some of the ryu's "no sword" techniques that an unarmed Yagyu bugeisha could use to overcome a weapon-wielding assailant. These are the very same techniques Muneyoshi had demonstrated so decisively to Iemitsu's grandfather years before to gain the Tokugawa lord's attention.

Again and again Munenori stepped in, cutting downward slowly with his bokken so that Iemitsu could practice disarming him. The shogun was able to twist the weapon from Munenori's grasp until Munenori increased the speed of the strike, and then Iemitsu would falter. The empty-handed muto techniques of the Yagyu Shinkage style required not so much in the way of oral instruction as they did in continuous practice to attain the perfect timing necessary to execute them. But the shogun was convinced that there was something Munenori wasn't showing him—some secret methods he left unrevealed. After all, his master had presented him with a certificate declaring that he had learned all the *shoden* and *chuden* teachings of the ryu, the basic and middle level techniques, so understandably, he felt he should be able to perform everything in the school's curriculum without fail.

To prove that Munenori was holding back instruction, Iemitsu decided to conduct an impromptu test. On the day after his lesson, he sent a request for his sensei to come to the Tokugawa mansion. When Munenori appeared, he was led by a servant to Iemitsu's quarters. Sliding back the shoji screen at the entranceway, Munenori dutifully dropped to his knees and bowed fully, his forehead resting on the tatami floor. The seated Iemitsu waited until his teacher was at the full length of the bow, then he snatched up a short spear from a weapon rack at his side and leaped at Munenori, driving the sharp point of the yari like a piston at the master. The shogun, like any other martial artist of his caliber, could stop his thrust perfectly, so he had no fear of hurting Munenori. He merely wanted to see how his teacher would put the day's lesson into a practical application. He saw. Still in a crouch, Munenori glided past the spear's tip and seized its shaft, using it as a fulcrum to swing his errant pupil up and onto the floor with an ignoble thump. Sheepishly, Iemitsu sat up and apologized, explaining why he had tried the stunt.

"No special secret," Munenori replied. "Just practice."

The Shogun Tokugawa Iemitsu went back to his training in swordsmanship without further complaint.

When the wealthiest and most influential figures of early Tokugawa Japan were introduced to Takuan the priest—and they were, for he consorted with them frequently throughout his life—they invariably noticed two things about him. One, he was eccentrically charismatic, remarkably so, and two, he was brilliant, impressively so.

Takuan Soho was born in 1573, the son of an impoverished *jizamurai* (a samurai retired, either by the death of his lord or a lack of funds to retain him, to the life of a country farmer). Like the male offspring of many poor families, Takuan was drawn to the security of the priesthood which, while it might not have provided much excitement or wealth, had the unmistakably attractive inducement of allowing one to eat regularly. Nine-year-old Takuan enrolled in a local temple of the Jodo sect of Buddhism, but four years later he left and requested entrance to the priesthood at the Zen temple Sukyo-ji.

While the boy Munenori was training with the sword and spear in the Shinkage style of the bujutsu at the dojo in Koyagyu, Takuan, three years younger, was receiving instruction in the arcane Buddhist sutras, submitting himself to the harshness of a cloistered existence. In addition, he was schooled in the tea ceremony and in calligraphy, arts considered necessary for the proper education of the Buddhist priest. It was a simple, often monotonous way of life, but Takuan's aptitude for it was proven by his posting, when he was only thirty-five years old, to the position of abbot of the great temple at Kyoto, Daitokuji.

To be appointed an abbot in the most venerable Zen temple in Japan at an age when most of his peers were still little more than temple servants for the elder priests was practically unheard of in the strict orders of the Buddhist clergy. Ieyasu was in the process of consolidating much of local governmental authority within the various Buddhist temples at that time, so it was also an advancement that could have meant for Takuan a rewarding amount of prestige and power within the shogunate's inner circles. After only three days at the office, however, Takuan resigned, disgusted with the politics and management duties that detracted from his studies and from the firsthand exposure to everyday life that was vital to the adherent of Zen. He took up the staff and the begging bowl, wandering from village to town as a mendicant monk.

Takuan's travels eventually took him to the hamlet of Yagyu while Munenori was still living there. He stopped in at the estate of the Yagyu lord Muneyoshi for several days, as he did at the homes of most of the daimyo when he passed through their provinces, to preach and give religious instruction. Yet, what began as just another stay at the home of a Nara lord became for both Takuan and Munenori the foundation for a lifelong friendship.

124

The essence of Zen, as Takuan saw it and as he taught it, was in the overcoming of ignorance which, he believed, was the principal hindrance to mankind's enlightenment, as well as a central reason for much of his suffering. The kind of ignorance Takuan addressed in his sermons and writings, though, was not that which sprung from a lack of technical or rational knowledge. He was concerned with the ignorance found in the preconceptions people have always held about life in any age or civilization, the random thoughts and fears and desires that in the philosophy of Zen are known as *bonno*. Bonno come in a variety of forms. For the feudal Japanese, just as for modern man, they could be in the anxieties of a dangerous situation like the battles faced by the samurai, or the dread of the unknown faced by a child entering school or by an old man on his deathbed. These preconceptions—preoccupations actually—restrict human existence, coloring it with shades that have no substance or value. For the bugeisha in the midst of combat, Takuan insisted, bonno can be fatal.

In everyday life, bonno prevent an individual from perceiving reality as it is, forcing him to live and experience his life filtered through the sieve of his own prejudices. By analogy, Takuan compared bonno to the leaves of a tree. If one's gaze stops on a single leaf, he fails to see it as a small part of the whole tree. In the same way, stopping the mind on an enemy's sword focused that faculty too intently and unobjectively, preventing a comprehension of the overall.

The solution to the many bonno of ignorance, Takuan maintained, was in the ceaseless cultivation of *mushin*. Often translated as "no mind," a clearer choice of words might be "non-abiding mind." Mushin was a subject of several letters and conversations between Takuan and Munenori, beginning with their meeting at Koyagyu. The non-abiding mind that Takuan urged his warrior friend to strive for he described as a state of consciousness that needs not ever stop to dwell on any particular phenomena. He insisted that to achieve mushin is to be aware of everything without being distracted by anything. The bugeisha entering a duel with this attitude had an objective awareness of his opponent and a sure knowledge of his own ability, since they are two of the "leaves" that make up the whole. In fact, he was also aware of the scores of other details the average swordsman wouldn't notice—things like, say, the direction of the sun's blindingly bright rays or the presence of a fallen branch that could cause a stumble during the fight. Yet, a fencer with mushin would refrain naturally and subconsciously from concentrating on any one detail, for he perceives them all, retaining what was useful to him, discarding from his thoughts that which was not, and continuing to keep his calmly balanced mind centered on the entire situation.

Because it is flowing constantly and not an artificially induced or static mentality, mushin works of its own accord, never upset by surprise or doubt. The priest wrote a long treatise in the form of a letter to Munenori and he titled it *Fudo Shinmyo Roku*, the "Record of Immovable Wisdom." Fudo, a protective, sword-bearing deity of Buddhism, symbolized for Takuan an unchanging wisdom that transcended time or circumstance. "Immovable," in the sense the Zen priest used it in his letter to Munenori, had the connotation of constancy and steadiness, for if mushin is authentic, Takuan believed it would be a quality permeating every moment of the martial artist's existence. Mushin, then, applied to a swordsman's activities whether they were related to the bujutsu or not. In the quality of his poetry, his calligraphy, his painting, or his sculpture, the warrior of mushin eloquently demonstrated his grasp of it.

In battle or duel, the bugeisha's uncluttered mind was expressed in the pure spontaneity of his fluid actions, a reflection of his Zen spirit. In his appreciation of everyday life, he expressed it with a preference for the simple, unaffected, and natural—an aesthetic sensitivity he shared with other artists. Once mushin was achieved, that which was extraneous or gaudily decorative was disdained; the bugeisha, acquiring a polished sense of perception, tended to regard them as contrary to the feeling of Zen. Seeking a reality stripped of artifice and illusion, searching for a way that elevated him beyond fears of death or an attachment to life, a swordsman possessing mushin was not concerned with outer ornamentation, but with an inner perfection. This was the message Takuan brought to Yagyumura and its bugeisha. Under his guidance, Munenori set about uniting the violence of swordsmanship with the tranquility of Zen, fusing the warrior's zanshin with the priest's mushin to seek that perfection in himself.

The friendship between Takuan and Munenori cemented through the years and it continued after Munenori left Yagyu village to become the retainer and fencing master to the Tokugawa family. In fact, it was their relationship that once saved Takuan from a lonely exile when the wayward and often outspoken priest had gotten himself into trouble with the Shogun Hidetada. The incident began when Takuan and two other abbots of Daitokuji journeyed to Edo for an audience with the shogun. (Though Takuan had resigned from his office as abbot, he still felt an allegiance to the temple and came to its aid when requested.) On behalf of Daitokuji, Takuan and the other abbots had gone to Edo to protest a recently enacted ruling of the shogun's giving him the right to commission the temple's chief abbot, a power that since the early fourteenth century had been reserved for the emperor himself. While it was a seemingly trivial matter, Hidetada resented the affront to his law and perhaps remembering the iron-handed political authority once wielded by Buddhist clergymen, his response to the complaint of the three Daitokuji priests had been to send all of them into exile.

Takuan might well have wiled away the remainder of his days in a rustic hut on the slopes of Kaminoyama, the "Mountain of the Gods," in a far-flung northeastern province, composing the Noh plays he loved and adding to his collection of Zen poetry. But Hidetada abdicated his position and died a few years after the exile, leaving Iemitsu as the next shogun. It was his karma, his fate, Takuan would undoubtedly have said, that not long after his appointment as shogun, Iemitsu happened to ask Munenori to what he attributed his skill in kenjutsu.

"I've followed the teachings of Takuan Soho," answered Munenori, a reply that so struck Iemitsu that he rescinded Takuan's order of banishment. In fact, at his sensei's urging, he invited the priest to visit him in Edo in 1635. The shogun was intrigued with Zen as Takuan explained it to him. Because he was Munenori's pupil and because Munenori was, in effect, a disciple of Takuan's, Iemitsu the mighty shogun sat and listened in humble silence while the priest and the swordsman talked. Zen is such a pragmatic school of thought that Takuan and Munenori could often include examples of how Zen philosophy could be applied to current politics and ordinary human affairs. On matters relating to taxation, military planning, or land use, Iemitsu benefited from the discussions of the two by learning to make the consistent, resolute decisions encouraged by the Zen mentality of the bugeisha and which were essential for the country to continue to prosper under his leadership.

Not all of Iemitsu's education in the way of Zen came from discussion. In the dojo, on hunting expeditions in the hills around Edo, or in court with his government, the shogun had an opportunity to see his sensei's philosophy in action. He could even encounter it at the theater.

The performance of Noh at the Edo castle was not a rare event. Noh, the stylized and subtle form of theater that the samurai naturally preferred to the more common and extravagant Kabuki that was enjoyed by the other classes, was staged several times a year at the Tokugawa castle. Even so, the appearance of Kanze Sakon, headmaster of the Kanze school of Noh and that art's most famous master, made the play a special occasion in the capital. Noh is the most ritualized of any theater form. A single gesture, a turning of the head or a lifting of the arm, can convey meaning of profound depth to the accomplished patron, so Noh actors had to train throughout their careers with painstaking thoroughness. To assume difficult poses and move with controlled, emotive grace, their strength and their mental concentration, their zanshin, had to be quite comparable to those of the bugeisha. It was, therefore, a matter of great interest for Munenori to watch Kanze on the stage. Invited to the play by Iemitsu, he studied the actor's movements with fervent attention. The shogun, sitting in front of Munenori, turned to him during a break in the play.

"Sensei," he whispered. "Is Kanze a man of zanshin? Does his concentration ever falter?"

Munenori squinted, as if considering the question, but made no comment.

128

"Please tell me then, if you see it broken in him during the play."

When the performance was ended, Munenori touched Iemitsu on the shoulder. "Kanze's zanshin is nearly flawless," he confirmed. "During the entire time he was on stage I saw him lose it only once, when he turned and sat near the pillar. At that moment he was without zanshin."

To Iemitsu's awestruck wonderment, he later discovered that while he was hearing Munenori's explanation of Kanze's performance, Kanze himself was speaking of it to one of his assistants in the dressing room behind the stage.

"There was a man sitting behind the shogun who was watching me with a ferocious intensity," he said. "Can you tell me who he was?"

"Of course," replied the assistant. "That was Lord Yagyu, the fencing master."

"Ah, that explains it then," Kanze said, nodding in understanding.

"What do you mean, master?" asked the puzzled assistant.

"My performance was a reasonably good one, but as I crouched during the scene by the pillar, my attention was distracted. It was only for an instant, yet as I turned toward the audience I saw Lord Yagyu smiling, as if he'd seen something missed by the rest. Indeed, he must have," Kanze finished to himself.

Indeed he had. Through the mental and physical challenges of a lifetime of training in the martial disciplines of the Yagyu Shinkage ryu and a commitment to the principles and philosophy of Takuan's Zen, Munenori's was an enlightened perception. His swordsmanship had gone far beyond mere technique and had become, like Zen itself, a thing of the spirit.

One morning a samurai named Jiro came to Munenori at the Edo Yagyu Shinkage dojo, requesting instruction in fencing. Since his kimono was the color of the Tokugawa clan, Munenori wondered why he hadn't enrolled at the school already, as most of the higher ranked Tokugawa bushi had done soon after Munenori was appointed as the shogun's instructor.

"Previously I was among the ranks of my lord's regular samurai," Jiro admitted. "But recently I was promoted to the palace guard and so I must improve my technique." He explained that his experience in kenjutsu had been rather limited and that he really knew very little about using the sword. Munenori led him to the main floor of the dojo, empty at the time, and with bokken in hand, the two took their places for a practice bout to give Munenori some idea of the samurai's level of ability.

The Yagyu master lifted his weapon into the chudan kamae, the middle posture taken in a training bout, but almost immediately he lowered it. "Why have you been dishonest with me?" he demanded of the samurai, who held his sword in front of him and could only look confused. "You said you knew only the basics of swordsmanship," Munenori pressed. "Yet obviously you are a master of it."

"No, Sensei," Jiro protested. "I know nothing about kenjutsu!" Munenori looked at him hard, his dark eyes burning from his scowl.

"You are a master," he insisted, and again the samurai denied it. "What then is it I sense about you?"

"I know of no reason why you would see anything in me," confessed Jiro. "I've always been a most ordinary sort, never accomplished at much. I suspect even my promotion was because of my father's reputation rather than anything I've done. The fact is," he went on, "I've never had the discipline to apply myself to a single thing except one."

Munenori looked at him thoughtfully. "What is that?"

"Early on, when I showed no aptitude for fencing or any other of the bujutsu, I concluded that as a bushi I would probably die in battle very quickly. Therefore, I spent all of my time contemplating my own death. I kept it in my thoughts constantly, no matter what I was doing. Over the years, it was an ever present companion, until I realized that I was no longer afraid to die. I have passed beyond any concern about it at all."

Munenori's questioning scowl faded. He went to a cabinet containing writing tools and took out a brush and paper for a certificate attesting to the samurai's capabilities. Stamping it with his seal and handing it to Jiro, he added, "There is nothing the bujutsu can teach you that you don't know already. To overcome life and death is to know the greatest of mastery."

11.
Lessons in the Warrior's Way

" . . . shibumi has to do with great refinement underlying commonplace appearances. It is a statement so correct that it does not have to be bold, so poignant it does not have to be pretty, so true it does not have to be real. Shibumi is understanding, rather than knowledge. Eloquent silence. In demeanour, it is modesty without pudency. In art, where the spirit of shibumi takes the form of sabi, it is elegant simplicity, articulate brevity. In philosophy, where shibumi emerges as wabi, it is spiritual tranquillity that is not passive, it is being without the angst of becoming. And in the personality of a man, it is . . . how does one say it? Authority without domination. Something like that."
Shibumi, *by Trevanian*

The Japanese game of go, among the oldest in the world, is a struggle of wit and style played out on a rectangular field of intersecting horizontal and longitudinal lines. To describe go in terms relatively as naive as referring to Wall Street's Crash of '29 as a business reversal, its intent is for each player to outline territory with his game pieces and to surround and restrict his opponent's territory. The playing pieces of go, placed on the board by the players in turn, are convex "stones" made of a dark black shale and milky white clamshell. Because they are just a bit too large to fit exactly on the board's interstices—unlike chess or checkers, go stones are set down where the squares on the board meet rather than in them—the game's appearance is one of a spontaneous irregularity that fits quite well with the Japanese identification with nature.

In a single afternoon, a person can be taught all the rules and concepts of go and in Japan, schoolchildren play it regularly. Despite the outer simplicity of the game, however, its strategy is of such an advanced nature that from the time it was introduced to Japan in the fifth century from neighboring China, gifted individuals of every class have devoted their lives to playing and mastering go. Even emperors and shoguns shared a passion for its complex challenges and the samurai pursued it as an excellent way to learn battlefield tactics.

In 1603, Honinbo Sansa, a virtuoso of the game, was appointed by the Shogun Tokugawa Ieyasu to head a government-sponsored go academy. Under the auspices of the academy, a system of grading participants like the one later used in the martial ways was instituted for go. Honinbo gave his name to his successor and it was passed on down the line for generations, a coveted title that was defended at matches before the emperor himself. In time, other renowned go families like the Hayashi and the Yasui rivaled the Honinbo clan for go supremacy, resulting in the technical advancement of go to a level of intricacy and sophistication not even dreamed of by aficionados of such comparatively mundane pastimes as chess.

The polished surface of the *goban*, the go board, is carved of *kaya* wood, with neatly plotted lines. The stones are black and white and seem in apparent disarray in the midst of battle. Even for the onlooker without any knowledge of its concepts and rules, go is a very beautiful game, a visual study in composition and color.

134

"Click." The white stone pinched between Kotaro Sensei's first and second fingertips he snapped onto the goban with a pleasant hollow sound that was enhanced by a deep slot cut on the underside of the board for just that purpose. As go's traditions demanded, my sensei, as the more skilled, was using the white stones. He had surrounded a formation of my black ones, leaving them with only one avenue of escape, which I took. Sensei's next stone cut off that route from the side, so once again I placed another stone above my previous play, hoping still to lead the group away from his crushing attack. Up, to the side, and up again, each time Sensei's white stones shut off my flight, hemming me in until I reached the edge of the board. In two moves, his stones surrounded mine and, leaving me without any freedom, he captured them, removed them from the game, and gave himself the points formerly occupied by them. I had lost the stones and the territory they protected by the play of *shicho*, a "ladder" that could only grow worse the more one gave up stones in an effort to save them. Although the beginner player believes he can beat out a shicho, inevitably he loses several stones and a great deal of territory for all his wasted effort.

Sensei's smile was faint as he scooped up my black stones and put them in the upturned lid of the bowl where they are stored. Our game took place in the summer kitchen of the house on the quiet street. Beside the table where we played the windows were pushed open and the cotton soft breezes of June ruffled the pages of magazines Mrs. Kotaro had stacked on a nearby cabinet.

"Once a mistake is made, it's no use to try to make up for it by adding on more," Sensei said as I reached to put down a stone in a far corner of the board. "Cut off the mistake, accept the loss, and go on. Same in go, same with Nixon, right?"

Though Sensei's tortured pronunciation of the president's name came out "Ni-ix-eyon," I got his point. Earlier I had asked my teacher how he felt about the then current political situation in which the president's reelection committee had apparently ordered a burglary and wiretapping of the headquarters of a rival party; the Watergate Scandal it was already being called. The president denied knowing about the break-in, but his denials had been followed by an unraveling string of admissions of guilt among his closest advisors, revealing a web of duplicity and coverup that were threatening the president with the alternatives of resigning or being impeached. Sensei muttered "so, des'ka'" when I sought his opinion and shrugged—it is not a trait of the Japanese to shrug and I liked to think that he had learned it from me—but he said nothing. Instead, he preferred to demonstrate to me what he thought of the Watergate affair, taking advantage of our game to do it.

My sensei, Ryokichi Kotaro, was a man of shibumi. Although he graduated from one of Japan's best universities to become an architectural engineer, an occupation demanding conversance in the most modern technology, his attitudes and personality were those of the bugeisha—a curious and not always compatible combination that was kept in order by the quiet and dignified aesthetic of shibumi. Sensei was not a man to force himself upon a situation. He did not order those around him, gave no hint of subservience to anyone, and displayed an almost quaint formality, even to close friends. His samurai ancestors had engendered him with a certain reserve that maintained a distance from the world around him. Sensei's approach to his own existence was a contemplative one, geared more to doing than to explaining himself. His approach to teaching me wasn't "do as I say, not as I do," but rather "do as I do, and nothing need be said at all." Accordingly, he rarely explained any of his beliefs to me in a straightforward, conversational way. Like my father, who let his behavior serve as the only guide for his children's conduct, he offered few lectures. Sensei preferred the obliquity of shibumi to express himself. He often used go to make analogies of life that were subtle and thought provoking, something go exponents who have reached the deeper levels of the game are likely to do. His go matches with me were also a form of instilling discipline, as well as another virtue Sensei valued, that of patience.

During go matches between masters, it isn't unusual for a player to spend several hours thinking out a move. The game that paired Master Shusai, the twenty-first Honinbo, with Kitani Minoru, took half a year to finish in 1938. This game was considered to be a pivotal meeting between the old classical style of go versus more recent innovations in the game. While there were recesses

136

that extended for weeks, delaying the completion of the game, the two participants were frequently sitting at the go board for seven or eight hours, lost in study.

Kotaro Sensei and I did not take that long in the occasional games we played, but he emphasized to me the need to sit quietly, perfectly still, to immerse myself in the flow of the game. If after twenty minutes or so of waiting for him to make his play, I took my eyes from the board, Sensei was sure to clear his throat in irritation, a warning that I should regain my concentration.

Go requires a symbiosis of mathematical reasoning and an imaginative foresight to deal correctly with problems that may come up several plays ahead. A stone placed in one corner of the board may seem inconsequential, but in later play it can suddenly assume a vital role. Further, the placement of stones and the style of play, the go masters say, is indicative of one's personal character. To an individual sensitive to the aesthetics of shibumi, it is possible to find the same courage, cunning, cowardice, or timidity that are encountered in swordsmanship. A folk legend has it that two expert bugeisha of old Japan met along a highway, argued over the merits of their ryu, and resolved to settle the argument with a duel. Both confessed to being hungry, however, so before they started, they went to an inn, ordered a meal, and decided to play a game of go afterward. Halfway through their game, the swordsmen looked up, in silent agreement. By the quality of their skill at the goban, each had demonstrated his character and ability. The duel with swords would have been superfluous.

While novice go players may get by with a reliance on simple logic or a flair for elementary strategy, to ever approach any sort of mastery of go requires shibumi, a grasp of the subtle and the unseen, a rarified capacity to express feeling or emotion with only a placement of a stone or by the manner in which it is snapped down on the board. Because shibumi is a sensation and a matter of aesthetics, it is inordinately difficult to describe. Whenever I mentioned it, Sensei would put his hand in front of his abdomen and push it outward, meaning that shibumi was something to be felt and not spoken of.

Soon after I began my bugei training, I started to learn go with

Sensei and it wasn't long until I realized that when he was showing me a particular tactic or a move, that often he meant for me to consider it in a far wider perspective than could be found within the confines of the go board. In one game, he demonstrated the fundamentals of *sente*, initiating plays that control an opponent's follow-up move, forcing him to make an answering counter play. In time, I was able to find this same kind of maneuvering in the dojo, where Sensei's mastery could direct all my efforts with the bokken, preventing me from ever taking the offensive, and limiting all my actions to responses, reactions that in the game of go are known as *gote*.

Sensei's lessons in sente and gote were of benefit to me away from the goban and the dojo, helping me to cope with many of the growing pains suffered by every adolescent. The social convulsions of the sixties were an uncertain environment for many of us and some reacted violently as they sensed the forthcoming toppling of outdated establishments. The unquestioned authority of teachers and school administrations was a monolithically stable fact of life in educating the youth of earlier decades, like a granite post office on the corner downtown that is of such imposing proportions that it's barely noticed for all its size. From Harvard to my own high school, though, venerated institutions of learning had settled and begun to fissure under their own weight, relenting too slowly to inevitable change. I encountered my share of the injustice and unresponsive complacency that were all too often the reasons for angry outbursts in classes, student demonstrations, and protests. Yet, with the examples set by the discipline of go, I learned that sometimes there is no choice but to respond to a difficult situation rather than to try impotently to dominate it, to survive and wait patiently to put oneself in a position to better control life, to be able to answer with the perseverance of gote until it is possible to play with the authority of a commanding sente.

The radical changes of the sixties were hardly confined to the halls of education, of course. It was in January of 1969 when I was 13, that full frontal nudity appeared in a popular magazine for the first time, in a dark and intriguing tangle of pubic fringe that peeked from the lap of a centerfold in the men's publication

Shambhala Publications, Inc.

Mailing List

P.O. Box 271

Boulder, Colorado 80306

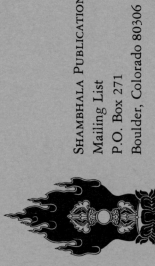

If you wish to receive a copy of the latest Shambhala Publications catalogue of books and to be placed on our mailing list please send us this card.

PLEASE PRINT

Book in which this card was found _____

Name: _____

Address: _____

City & State: _____

Zip or Postal Code: _____ Country (if outside U.S.A.): _____

Playboy. Actually, it was little more than a single shot amidst the barrage, for in a war fought with ammunition as unlikely and diverse as miniskirts, the Pill, and love-ins, the Sexual Revolution had swollen into almost a crusade during that decade of the daringly new and unconventional. Sexuality was burgeoning, blossoming; I saw it in the girls I went to school with and in the defiant attitudes of movies and the theater. (I had a matronly English teacher who never quite recovered from a summer holiday in Manhattan where she saw *The Graduate* and *Oh, Calcutta* in the same day.) Sexuality was bursting to ripeness around those of us growing up then, enveloping our senses in a musky perfume that tantalized and dared. While the demands of my almost daily training did keep me from backseat fumbling at the local drive-ins and even from much tentative fondling on parents' sofas, I wasn't exempt from the revolution's call to arms, nor was my experience in the bujutsu unaffected by the lure of its lusty battles. On the contrary, my tutoring in that area was well tended to, and, as most things in my life were then, it was tinged with the poignancy of long ago Japan.

Like most older Japanese who were from sexually tolerant rural backgrounds and were of the generations before Western influences were so prevalent there, Kotaro Sensei and his wife Kaoru were rather casual about the whole thing. Kaoru was unaffectedly careless about nudity and I frequently caught glimpses of her gently sloping breasts and chocolate nipples when her *yukata* (bathrobe) was loosely tied after a soak in the upstairs tub. Sensei never brought the subject up directly, but he spoke without embarrassment about sex, usually implying that, as with the bujutsu, the arts of love were to be conscientiously practiced and refined by the bugeisha, and in that field too, more was expected of him than of the ordinary person.

"Tsuki no sen geiko, tsuki no sen seiko," he once matter of factly reminded me when my arms seemed too tired to make even one more strike with the bokken.

"Hai!" I returned, filled with fresh enthusiasm. Sensei had quoted a traditional adage of the Yagyu Shinkage ryu: "A thousand thrusts in martial arts practice and a thousand thrusts in making love are the ingredients for making an individual of character." I wasn't sure what kind of pep talks my athlete schoolmates were getting from their coaches in football and track, but I was reasonably certain they couldn't have compared.

One afternoon at the university library, I came across a book of *shunga*, the colorful, explicitly sexual woodblock prints that were popular in Japan during the feudal age. The text, written in unintelligible Japanese, to my dismay, was full of the most acrobatically involved couples I had ever seen, and given the trends in movies and magazines of that era, I had seen a lot. To be confronted with the most delightful prints and to be unable to read any of the lengthy and, I was convinced, graphic captions, put me in a frustrating spot. With little hesitation I checked the book out and headed for the house on the quiet street, confident that Sensei or Kaoru-san would be able to decipher them for me.

Kaoru sat down with me and laughed when I noted the enormous phalluses of the males in the prints. I had been in the gym showers at the university with my sensei and with other Japanese students who practiced with the judo club often enough to know that such dimensions existed only in the ambitious imaginations of the woodblock artists, but Kaoru explained to me that giant genitalia weren't the object of the prints. Instead, she showed me the gracefully arranged limbs of the couples, especially those of the women. Even in the throes of what looked like wondrously fascinating stuff, the women of the shunga prints had a sublime sort of grace, with even their fingers and toes carefully arranged to achieve a subtle eroticism that was far more exciting, once it was pointed out, than the more obvious act of penetration and reception. Kaoru explained that the ability to project this delicate style was a particular manifestation of shibumi called *shiseido*, the "way of femininity," a cultivated presence of sensuality that required the same aesthetic sensitivity to appreciate as was necessary for mastering go. As for the males in the prints, though they were busily engaged in postures Sensei's wife translated as "The Tiger Plunging into the Stream," "Tugging at the Willow Bough," and so on, they depicted a similar kind of grace, a lithe gentleness that was difficult for Kaoru to put into words. It was a masculine form of shiseido, she said, that was referred to admiringly as *bushi no nasake,* the "tenderness of the warrior."

"Lotsa time see sex in movies now," Kaoru waved in dismissal. "Only in-yo, in-yo, yame." (In and out, in and out, and the end.) "No shisei, no nasake. This almost no better than animals. Like have itching and must scratch, neh?" She made it clear that sex without shibumi was like sex without emotional involvement; empty and shallow and beneath the consideration of an "individual of character."

I do not believe any women anywhere are possessed of more beautiful and supple hands than those of the Japanese woman. In the shunga prints, those hands excited, stroked, and urged—the essence of feminine grace, the epitome of shibumi in their restrained subtlety. They have their own strength and rhythms, and, given the rampant sexuality of the day that seemed but a scratching of an itch, I knew I was most fortunate in that it was from hands such as those that I was taught my lessons in the gentleness of the bugeisha.

The philosophical and the practical: my education as a student of the Yagyu Shinkage tradition seemed to be an endless combination of both that were distinct at one level of examination and then merged and flowed together at another. In the dojo, the sword was an instrument for taking a life and so I trained constantly, learning to use it to cut down an enemy, a study not any the less detailed despite the fact that it would almost certainly never be put to use. More than once a bokken was splintered as Sensei made every effort to impress upon me the need for the bugeisha to maintain the exacting standards of the feudal bujutsu, keeping in the forefront of my practice an accent on correct form and action. While a throw in judo could be adapted to the practitioner's body or style of attack once he had learned it well, the techniques of the bujutsu, as a historically true legacy of the past, had to be preserved precisely as they were taught. As much as possible they had to be practiced as they were centuries ago; to do otherwise would be as unthinkable as sawing the arms off a Windsor chair to make it lighter to move about. To infer that this was the ultimate aim of the Yagyu Shinkage ryu, however, would be a very limited view of the classical martial arts.

Kotaro Sensei was at the dining room table, writing a letter to a friend back in Japan one day. Normally when he wrote letters in Japanese, he used a felt-tipped pen to make the syllabic shorthand of modern Japanese writing, but because this correspondence was more formal, Sensei was writing in the much older *kanji* characters of Japanese script with ink and a soft bristled brush. There is a maxim in the bujutsu, *ken, shu, ichi,* a reminder that the katana and the brush are one and the same in practice and the swordsman must wield his blade with exactly the accuracy and artistry with which he employs a brush to render the intricate characters of calligraphy. Sensei's characters, like his swordsmanship, were adroit and flowing, unconsciously expert. I sat in the chair beside him, watching, and when he had finished the letter, he handed me his brush and told me to show him what I had learned from the calligraphy books I had been looking through.

"Satsujinken," I brushed on a sheet of clean paper, my strokes drawn too carefully, without the ease of my teacher's and showing it in their slightly off-balanced structure and clumsy spacing.

"What's this mean?" Sensei stretched back, propping his chair up on its rear legs, folding his arms across his chest.

"Satsujinken," I said. "The sword that takes life, the sword that kills."

Sensei pursed his lips. "Important for the bugeisha to have this kind of sword?" he asked.

I nodded.

Kotaro Sensei leaned forward and brought the chair back down on all its legs. He took the brush from me, swirled it in the wet ink that was pooled at the end of his little square inkstone and beside my characters he wrote *katsujinken,* "the sword that gives life."

"This is even more important, I think," he said.

"Katsujinken, satsujinken" is an adage that has been brushed on inspirational scrolls hung in Yagyu ryu dojo and on certificates and teaching licenses awarded to its bugeisha. It is found in the treatises written by Munenori and others. More importantly than anywhere else, katsujinken, satsujinken must be inscribed on the hearts of the practitioners of the ryu. In a way, it is at the very core of what the Yagyu tradition is all about.

Satsujinken, the sword that destroys human life, was a common enough weapon among the bujutsu exponents of old. When a disciple apprenticed himself to a ryu to learn kenjutsu, his aim was almost invariably to make himself into a more efficient fighter. Upon reaching this level of skill, the majority were content to remain there as nothing more than technicians. Their intent was to win, or at least to avoid dying, so they trained to be better than anyone they might happen to meet in combat. If they were successful in the endeavor, they prevailed and survived. If not, they died. Many a swordsman achieved his fame not through the defeating of a string of opponents in spectacular dueling, but from having the circumspection to challenge only those he was reasonably certain of beating, avoiding industriously the rest. It was not a wholly inadvisable course for the professional martial artist to take, for the stakes were terribly high. When he was drawn into a fight, the bugeisha was fully aware that there could only be one of three conclusions: he could kill his opponent, he could be killed, or both he and the opponent could be struck down in the same instant.*

To kill, be killed, or to die in a mutual slaying—these were the choices for the bugeisha. Had they remained the only outcomes possible in his life, he would, no doubt, have assumed a role in history no better than that of any other warrior of any other culture. He would have been a purveyor of death. But from the swordsmanship of the Yagyu Shinkage school, with its foundations sunk deeply in the ancient mysticism of Shinto and Buddhism and its structure buttressed by the pragmatic earthiness of Zen, arose a different alternative to the bugeisha's dilemma. Instead of the purely physical conflict with an opponent, the masters of the Yagyu ryu

*It was, incidentally, the latter in which the bugeisha often met his end, for the fractional space and timing between life and death were so awfully close as to be inseparable.

understood that the real conflicts of existence come within oneself, in the soul and the psyche of a man as he grapples with his own mortality—and morality—in the dark corners of his self that no opponent could ever reach. These were the inner fields of battle, swordsmen of the Yagyu style of fencing were taught, where the life of the bugeisha was won or lost, for it was in that secret place that he forged for himself either just another life, or a life that was worthy of living.

To strike and kill an enemy was, for men like Yagyu Munenori, simply an implementation of technique. It was karma that decided victory or defeat. It was the art of the sword in its basest capacity. But the challenge presented by the self was another matter entirely. Throughout a man's years on earth, his spirit is destined to be assailed by the doubts, the fears, and the desires that will never leave him in peace unless he overcomes them. For the corporeal opponents of flesh and blood and steel that he faced in duels, the Yagyu bugeisha reserved his satsujinken, the sword that took life.

For the battles that went on inside, though, he needed a much stronger weapon, with a keener blade perhaps than even the mythical sword Susa-no-o-in-izumo snatched from the belly of the eight-headed dragon so many centuries ago in Japan's past. This is the sword he called katsujinken, the sword that gives life.

The transformation of the sword in the bugeisha's hands from a weapon that takes life to one that grants it is a long and arduous process. The process cannot even be attempted without an immersion into the fundamentals of swordsmanship that force an exponent to come face to face with an opponent often enough so that eventually, it is hoped by his sensei, he will come to face himself. The method is not easy, particularly because every encounter leads only to further challenge. For every question answered about myself through the rigors of the bujutsu, another score arose.

There were moments in my training, too many to count, when Sensei's bokken came slashing at me and I thought with the merest periphery of my consciousness about the parry and counter. The center of my attention was taken with my own limitations, and I wondered how much more I could take. From the moment I had stepped into the dojo, I began a struggle with the boundaries, imposed by my mind, that threatened and bullied at every step to overwhelm me. "I wasn't meant for this," the voice inside me would cry. I was a Westerner, I wasn't strong enough to take the punishment. I fought a dozen duels with myself for every cut I made with the katana. Sometimes I won, sometimes not. The nights when I won over myself and pushed back the limitations a bit, I would jump down under the stone bridge in the park on my way home, full of confidence and contentment, rubbing my sore muscles briskly, reveling in the whole specialness of being a part of the classical martial arts. But there were other nights, many others, when I crept down under the bridge, tucked my arms around my legs, and stained the knees of my jeans with tears. The weariness that made me stop beneath the bridge in the park was often not a physical one, for the bujutsu were making me decidedly healthy, free from most sicknesses or even minor sniffles and colds. I would have to pause to rest and put my head in my arms because of the fatigue of my spirit and the horrible, shameful thought that I could go no further.

I cannot say exactly why I didn't quit. Maybe it was because after a while I came to feel that I wasn't involved in the struggle alone. There wasn't any illuminating flash of enlightenment. It was just that gradually I grew to suspect, and then to believe, that I was another link in a chain that I could not really add to or detract from; I could only take my place along with all the rest who had preceded me in the ryu. It was a feeling that was germinated after one of the few instances when Kotaro Sensei spoke to me at length about the philosophy of the bugeisha.

During the day, intent-faced dance students in leotards and leg warmers flexed and bounced in the huge, cathedral-ceilinged room that was off the main gym of the university, a building larger than a basketball court with nothing in it but a wooden floor, ballet barres along one wall, and the pungent odor of rosin and sweat. In the evenings, it was empty and occasionally we left the dojo to go and train there. It was on such an evening, thick with the heat of August's summer, that Sensei and I had performed kata.

The basics and middle level kata were instinctive now; I ran through their motions with the assurance that came from constant repetition. Even when Sensei changed the sequence of the movements, switching from one kata to another without warning, I could keep up and respond to his actions correctly. Blows that once would have knocked me completely off my feet I could now absorb and deflect, and return with a focused attack of my own. Even when his movements went beyond the kata and became spontaneous, I could successfully counter many of them. He would flick the sword up at my hands—in theory a small, rapid stroke that would have chopped off my thumbs and rendered me incapable of holding the sword and making further defense—and I could smack the wooden blade aside before it reached the target. I would come back, faking a slash at his head, then stabbing with the point of my bokken aimed at his chest, then executing a vertical cut. Sensei's parries, while they weren't exercised to even a half of their fullest capability, let me know that I was making progress, moving from the position of the beginning student into the realm of the matured swordsman.

When the smothering swelter of the dance room became too much for us to continue, we stripped out of our hakama and jackets, showered, and then we went out to perch on the high steps of the gym, lazing on the smooth coolness of the limestone. We were like a pair of plantation barons surveying our domain, except that instead of cotton fields, below and in front of us spread a wide green lawn, the hedges, and the sidewalks of that part of the campus. On the opposite side of the lawn, a street of sedate old houses seemed to squat and sprawl gratefully beneath the shade of enormous trees that gave out their shade in a limp and listless way during the height of the day's humidity, awaiting the dark that was now coming, to breathe into their limp leaves a draw of rejuvenating night air.

Our walk from his house on the quiet street to the university took us by a small cemetery. Sensei had been describing to me the gravestones that were in cemeteries in Japan, how their tiered construction was a representation of the five elements—earth, air, fire, metal, and water—that symbolized the cosmos in Taoist lore. We resumed the subject again after training, but we were both hot and lethargic from our session and the conversation dwindled. From

146

behind the clumped crowns of the trees a cloud ballooned up. It was bright white around the edges, catching the last rays thrown out by the setting sun. Its fat belly was gray and expanding, not as a threat yet, but as more a suggestion of the storm it presaged. As other clouds followed the first, each equally ponderous with the portent of a summer thundershower, a hesitant burst of wind stuttered across the campus. It dried the dampness of the shower that still clung to my shirt and I drowsily stretched and yawned. The breeze seemed to stir Sensei into thought and he started to speak again, apparently with our earlier conversation still in mind. His words were measured and carefully selected and as always, I was surprised at how well he could express himself in English when he wished to do so.

"The Americans say of the Japanese that we 'worship' our ancestors. I suppose in a way we do, but differently from worship, we believe we are a part of our ancestors. If we do or do not do a thing, it is influenced by how we believe our ancestors would view it."

Another gust skidded over the campus, bowing the smaller branches of the trees, kicking up the dust that had collected along the brick-lined streets near the university.

"American society is well meaning," Sensei said. "Americans can be kind and generous. They are sometimes simple thinking; they want so much to be equal to one another in all ways. But they have built a civilization on that principle, so it isn't so bad at all for them." He was quiet for a moment, slotting his thoughts into sentences. "If there is anything that Americans don't have, it is a feeling . . . a *sense* of the past. They learn about the past in history books and it is something that affects them in an unimportant way, they believe."

There was a rumble, very faint, that could have been thunder when Sensei spoke again. "The swordsmanship we do, that is nothing. What is cutting with a sword? If I have an atomic bomb now, it will melt your katana and you, just push a button from a thousand miles away."

"We keep the Yagyu Shinkage tradition alive for another reason than fighting. Because it is like—" he paused, reaching for the right word, "it is like an *antique* that is living. Because we have

147

the ryu, we have something of the past. We can depend on it. All the bugeisha in the old days, they are just like us. Same problems, they loved and hated, just like we do. Since they went before, they are an example for us. We must never forget that we are a part of them."

What Sensei was explaining to me was *nakaima*, the "eternal present," the timelessness that links the classical martial artist with those who have preceded him. In the kata and rituals of the bujutsu, the spirit of the bugeisha's philosophy is retained through the successive generations like a precious heirloom. This connection gives to the bugeisha of the present the forbearance to create for himself a life that perceives quality in simple things, that encourages him to face others as honestly as he faces himself, that allows him a sense of purpose and stability in a world constantly changing. Because his present is so deeply nurtured and fortified by the ways of the past, his character is polished by it and he is refined into a person of value to his society, a possessor of the life-giving katsujinken. He becomes a man of shibumi.

The clouds were lowering, too full of rain to bear their burden so high in the sky. And the breeze was stronger now, rocking whole branches when it struck, whooshing away the humidity, leaving the air fresh and moist. It was time for us to go home, Sensei said, before the rain came, so we gathered up our bokken and the bags that held our training clothes and walked down the street as the shadows of the sunset were lost in the dark of the coming storm.

Sensei was right. In an hour or so, it would begin to rain.

The remains of the Yagyu mansion in present-day Nara Prefecture.

12.

Things Out of Season

The final decade in the life of Yagyu Tajima no kami Munenori was taken up with teaching and with an introspective analysis of the craft of swordplay. With a reputation exceeding that of any swordsman in Japan and with his position as a confidant and sensei to the shogun fully established, Munenori no longer had to prove his abilities in combat or duel. He was free to devote himself utterly to the symbiosis of Zen and swordsmanship. Servants who attended to Munenori in his old age frequently caught sight of him in his garden, absolutely motionless, sword in hand, occupied not with the physical mechanics of posture and movement but with the abstruse precepts of Takuan's Zen that elevated the bujutsu from technique to a medium of spiritual contemplation. From his efforts and the accumulated experience of a lifetime came a treatise of Munenori's insights, the *Heihokadensho*.

Within the pages of the *Heihokadensho*, which may be translated simply as a "Chronicle of Strategy," are the author's flowing calligraphy and the spindly stick figures engaged in battle he drew with the brush, instructions meant for use by the swordsmen of the Yagyu Shinkage ryu. Typical of bujutsu texts that were written only as a form of hints or suggestions for the student and never as an explicit guide, the treatise is couched in a style of shorthand language that makes it difficult for modern readers to fully understand all the contents—the fear of rival schools or unscrupulous individuals perverting the intentions of the ryu kept headmasters like Munenori from being too free in their writings—and for someone uninitiated in the basic methods of the Yagyu tradition, a grasp of the book's secrets is impossible. It is filled with esoteric references like the "Eye of the Dragonfly" and strategies such as the mental spirit that is like "the white waves left by the moving ship." Several passages are quite clear and straightforward, however, because Munenori intended them to be a kind of explanation of the way of the bugeisha. One introductory section is devoted to the attitude he believed the Yagyu Shinkage swordsman should adopt in life, and when the deeper meaning of this passage is taken into account, it can be seen as a summation of what Munenori knew was the only manner in which a martial artist could conduct himself if he wished to be anything more than a swordsman of satsujinken.

"The warrior is an ill-fated instrument," he wrote. "The way of the gods has no use for him, yet must make use of him, for that is the way of Heaven." Heaven's employment of the bugeisha, according to Munenori, was used to the fullest when he consciously pursued a path of moral rectitude. "Ten thousand are oppressed by the wickedness of a single man and by killing that one man the ten thousand are given new life. There is righteousness in using the *heiho* (the tactics of a bujutsu ryu) this way. Without righteousness, it is simply a question of killing other people and avoiding being killed by them. Consider carefully what martial strategy really is."

In the late winter of 1646 the Shogun Tokugawa Iemitsu came to Munenori's home in Azabu and with the formality and bearing of someone of his noble rank, he was led into the bedroom of

Munenori, where his master lay dying at the age of 78. It required two of the headmaster's attendants to lift his rapidly weakening body into a sitting position, but once there, Munenori calmly gave his final instruction to the shogun in the style of the Yagyu Shinkage school of fencing. Iemitsu, whose father the great Ieyasu had once remarked that if the Tokugawa reign was to prosper "its government must be run according to the principles and philosophy of the Yagyu Shinkage ryu," listened silently to his teacher as tears began to cloud and sting in his eyes. At the end of the last lesson, Iemitsu bowed, lowered himself fully to the tatami. From his propped-up position, Munenori returned the bow with a slight nod. It was the proper way between sensei and student, even if the sensei was a transplanted country rustic and his student, the shogun of Japan.

In a matter of hours following his final lecture to Iemitsu, Munenori died, almost exactly three months after the death of his own master, Takuan Soho. He was buried, at the shogun's orders, with the honors afforded a hatamoto. Along with his father's and other members of the Yagyu clan's graves, his grave is in the shady cemetery of the Hotokuji, the temple that served the population around and in Yagyumura and still houses the original, handwritten version of Munenori's *Heihokadensho*, along with several other writings, weaponry, and heirlooms of the family.

Munenori's grave overlooks the hamlet where both he and his ryu were born. Off on a nearby hilltop stands the rock foundation of Koyagyu, all that remains of the clan's mansion. In the village below it, farmers continue to raise rice and barley as they did in Munenori's day. A little farther beyond the village, in a glen surrounded by maple and bamboo, is a huge boulder, split neatly in half. It is a stone locally famous for many generations, for as Yagyumura folktales have it, its fissure is the result of a duel Munenori's father Muneyoshi had with a mountain goblin one night long ago. Muneyoshi, legend has it, missed the goblin in one ferocious cut, splitting open the boulder instead.

It is fitting, Munenori might have thought, that at the foot of the wooded hill below his grave now stands the Masakisaka Dojo, where twentieth-century boys gather to train and sweat in the dis-

151

cipline of the sword. Their weapons are not the steel katana or even the dangerous bokken, but the bamboo shinai, the modern equivalent of Kamiizumi Nobutsuna's wood and leather fukuro shinai. Their training is not in kenjutsu, the *art* of the sword, but in kendo, the *way* of the sword. Although they are not of the Yagyu Shinkage ryu, of course, in their efforts toward reaching self-perfection with the sword, they would, no doubt, have been a most gratifying sight to a warrior of katsujinken like Yagyu Munenori.

After Munenori's death in 1646, his son Yagyu Jubei Mitsuyoshi took his place as headmaster of the ryu in Edo. Though he lacked his father's genius, Jubei was a bugeisha of considerable philosophical convictions. Before he assumed control of the ryu, Jubei spent twelve mysterious years as a *sometsuke*, a secret agent of sorts, for the shogun. His adventures during these dark years remain largely unknown, but stories of the clandestine assignments he carried out in the service of the shogun have long been fictionalized favorites of readers in Japan. Under his guidance as headmaster of the ryu, the Yagyu Shinkage style flourished and grew. Jubei continued in his father's role as fencing teacher and advisor to Iemitsu until four years later when he died unexpectedly— but peacefully—in 1650.

When Yagyu Jubei ascended to leadership of the Yagyu Shinkage style of the bujutsu, he inherited only one half of the ryu, for in the early part of the sixteenth century, it had split into two different sects. The eldest son of Muneyoshi, Yagyu Yoshikatsu, had been denied headmastery of the school and the appointment to be the shogun's instructor because of the crippling wound he had suffered in a battle years before. However, despite his handicap, Yoshikatsu persisted in his training in swordsmanship in the dojo at Koyagyu, where he instructed his son Toshiyori as well.*

The instruction must have been good: in 1615, Toshiyori became the fencing master to Tokugawa Yoshinao, a distant relative

*Yagyu Toshiyori was also sent by his father to his uncle, Munenori, where he received the attention that allowed him to attain mastery of swordsmanship while he was still quite young.

of the shogun's and the daimyo of Owari Province. Although the differences between the Yagyu style as it was taught in the Edo dojo of Munenori and that which was carried on in Yagyu village after he left, were slight, it was Toshiyori's intention to establish himself separately and so he referred to his school as the Owari or Bishu (Orthodox) Yagyu Shinkage ryu. Even though the two schools emerged as distinct, they shared the common tradition that had been bred in the mountains of the Kinki area.

From the Edo and Owari Yagyu Shinkage styles of the bujutsu came enough expert swordsmen and their exploits to fill many volumes. There was Yagyu Hida no kami Munefuyu, who was said to be able to jump nearly eight feet in making awesome overhead slashes that bisected his opponents like a stroke of lightning descending from above.* Yagyu Toshikane Renyasai was as renowned for the craftsmanship of his sword guards as he was for his skill at kenjutsu. A legend has it that he forged several guards and then, wishing to test them for durability, he put them all in a cauldron and proceeded to pound away at them with a heavy mallet. Only those that survived the beating intact he judged worthy of his name. (Many exist today, prized by collectors and museums.)

In Owari and Yagyumura, the orthodox style of the ryu was maintained by hardy and determined generations of bugeisha. In Edo, the descendants of Yagyu Munenori kept the school healthy, their headmasters remaining as instructors to the shoguns until the Meiji Restoration in 1867. In fact, the stage was set for the end of the Yagyu's reign of distinction when, in the turmoil of the Restoration, a young, ambitious Emperor Meiji disbanded the Tokugawa shogunate to replace it with Japan's first alteration in government in over three centuries.

Prior to the Emperor Meiji's abolishment of feudalism, there had been a rivalry between the two sects of the Yagyu Shinkage ryu. The Owari practitioners insisted that Munenori had made changes in technique and curriculum that, while not vital, were nonetheless an alteration of the fundamental nature of the ryu. The

---

*Yagyu Munefuyu, the brother of Jubei, became the next headmaster of the Edo school after Jubei's death.

Edo swordsmen denied the accusation and let their bokken, and occasionally, their katana provide their school's defense in duels and challenges that occurred intermittently from the last years of the 1600s until the end of the 1800s. But when the emperor launched his nationwide plans for modernization of the country, the feud erupted into a more serious one.

Naturally, not all of Japan was eager for the massive changes envisioned by the emperor. There were those who wanted to retain the old form of rule under the Tokugawa shoguns and who despised any of the accommodations to the Western world that were sweeping through Japan at an astonishingly rapid rate. Others, particularly those out of favor with the Tokugawa regime or oppressed by the restraints of economic feudalism, looked forward to the opportunities presented by new ways. On the outer fringes of each faction were adamant proponents and fanatical supporters, ready to die for their causes. Not surprisingly, both sides included in their ranks a number of bugeisha, armed and spoiling for a fight.

Members of the Edo and Owari Yagyu Shinkage ryu found themselves on both sides, some supporting the emperor, others the shogunate. As the products of a warrior culture, it was inevitable that they would defend their beliefs with their lives, sword in hand. And so once more the hillsides and forested roads along the valleys around Yagyumura rang with the reverberations of swords in combat, but this time it was the bugeisha of the land fighting not some outside invader, but one another. Their duels were fierce and deadly, fueled by the emotionally charged issues of the Restoration. The cobblestone highways that wound through that part of the Kinki region became smeared with Yagyu blood. At the roadsides, in mute testimony, sprouted carved gray stones that marked the final resting places of the stalwart bugeisha of the Yagyu ryu.

It is this explanation that is customarily presented by historians as the reason for the almost complete demise of the Yagyu family and their style of swordsmanship (as well as for the similar extinction of many clans and bujutsu ryu during that time). They simply and very nearly totally wiped each other out, their losses barely noticed in the social upheaval of the period. Only a few dozen practitioners

154

were left to carry on with the ryu's traditions. But it was also the end of an age that signaled the eclipse of the Yagyu Shinkage school, and the dawning of a new era that had scant need for the feudal institution of the ryu system or the violent ways of the classical martial exponent. The day of the samurai—and the bugeisha—was over.

Of course, the swordsmanship of the Yagyu family did not become extinguished entirely. Men who cared more for its philosophy and ethics than for its murderous techniques passed on the teaching with the loving respect with which outstanding individuals have always regarded something of value. It remains so today. Yet from the final decade of feudalism in Japan until the present, its adherents have known that their practice has an air of subdued sadness about it. Their rituals and skills, demonstrated for the public now on occasion at special exhibitions in Japan, are exciting and a dramatic reminder for the audiences of their country's history. The perceptive observer can feel, though, that there is an unmistakable melancholia underneath it all. While the modern-day disciples of the ryu draw their katana and slash at the invisible enemies about them or smash their bokken together in the parries and attacks of the kata, there is a sense of quiet somberness in their movements. Perhaps it is only the quality of their shibumi, but it is as if they are resigned to some fate they know all too well, remembering the words of Abe Shosaburo, a master swordsman of the ryu who had his own idea about why the bugeisha of the Yagyu Shinkage tradition met their deaths in such a bloody way during the Restoration.

"In the changing of the times," Abe wrote to one of his students, "they were like autumn lightning, a thing out of season, an empty promise of rain that would fall unheeded on fields already bare."

The Masakisaka Dojo in Yagyu village, where descendants of the Yagyu family's retainers still train in kendo, the modern equivalent of classical swordsmanship.

Afterword

The glossy lacquered armor of the samurai rests in its glass-fronted case, still lustrous after all these years, the braided silk cord bindings still bright. The swords curving in their racks, blades up, have not lost their sharpness or the polish of their finish, the time-consuming work of craftsmen centuries ago still in evidence. There are spears eight feet and longer, their points and bladed barbs as frightfully honed as ever. And there are powerful arrows with reed shafts and chrome-shiny heads with razor edges and Sanskrit designs engraved lovingly on their sides. Gracefully bent bows of mulberry and bamboo are still strung as if ready to be picked up and drawn. It is like the armory of some ancient daimyo's castle. There are the flat, pan-like jingasa head coverings; the bucket-shaped helmets with their fierce crescent horns of brass; and the *menpo*, the masks that shielded their wearers' throats and protected their lower faces, masks that now grimace emptily and mouth silent cries of battle.

The display of the samurai's armament is one of the most extensive in any collection, but it is not in some repository in Japan. It is at the Peabody Museum, on Essex Street, in the middle of Salem, Massachusetts, a staggeringly voluminous array brought back from Japan at the first part of the last century by ship captains when Salem was the foremost clipper ship port in the world.

There is a sensation of that which is shibumi for me to walk through the halls containing the Japanese collection at the museum on Essex Street and to continue on to the rooms beside them that house the reminders of the great sailing days of old Salem: flamboyantly painted figureheads; a Swampscott dory, lines coiled in her bilges and shipshape to be put to work fishing for cod on St. Georges Banks; an enormous miscellany of scrimshaw and harpoon irons. From a story-high Korean fertility totem to a tiny porcelain drinking cup used by caged singing crickets in China, they are here—all of the exotic knicknacks that the deepwater men of Salem brought back with them as they plied the oceans of faraway places.

The halls of the museum hold so much of the two cultures that have shaped and geared me. In one room, I can admire the paintings of whaling ships like those on which my great grandfather worked. I can run a finger along the cool steel of the big harpoons that were stabbed through the smooth wet backs of those giant creatures of the waves. And then, in another room are the swords and the armor that my ancestors in the bujutsu used in their own battles, their elegantly simple artwork, and the everyday things of their lives. In Salem, at the Peabody Museum, are both tributaries of my pasts and whenever I wander through its wide halls, the orts and treasures of both cultures all about me, I cannot help but reflect on the dual heritage that I have acquired.

Perhaps like in the museum, the Oriental and Occidental will be in separate places within me, the two heritages together and yet apart, never mingling. I hope not, for I suspect that it will be a measure of the legacies both ancestors left for me that the two can flow inside me, accentuating the contrasts where they occur and melding ever more strongly when they coincide. In both East and West, in every generation, those who have preceded me have been confronted with challenges, and it seems this is to be one of mine:

to mold my pasts into a single present, into a single soul. It is not an easy task, of course, but then again, I must always bear in mind that, as my sensei warned me on an afternoon when I first set out on this way, more is expected of a bugeisha.

Glossary

ai (coming together, unity)   A basic principle of the martial arts and ways, involving the relationship between, for example, mind and body, body and weapon, attacker and defender.

battojutsu A name preferred by some traditional schools of martial arts for the techniques of the fast sword draw. (See *iaijutsu*.)

bokken The wooden sword, similar in size, shape, and weight to the Japanese steel sword. The bokken is used in practice sessions to avoid injury.

budo The collective name for the "martial ways." The primary emphasis of budo is the character development of practitioners. Evolving from the bugei at the end of the feudal era, the modern budo include judo, karate-do, aikido, kendo, and kyudo.

bugei (martial arts) The classical martial arts as originally practiced during the age of the samurai. The bugei are still maintained in a minor way for historical and aesthetic purposes. Practically speaking, the bugei are synonymous with the bujutsu.

bugeisha A practitioner of the bugei.

bujutsu (martial arts) The classical martial arts of Japan, also called the bugei. The bujutsu include kenjutsu (fencing), sojutsu (the art of the spear), bojutsu (the art of the staff), and a variety of martially oriented disciplines. The bujutsu are distinguished from the budo by their more ancient roots and by their emphasis on actual combat.

buke A family of samurai rank, or a clan of samurai.

bushi Another name for the samurai, or warrior, of feudal Japan.

bushi damashi (warrior spirit) The emotional essence of the martial arts, demonstrated through simplicity in everyday life, rigorous training, and constant reflection on one's progress. Bushi damashi is expressed by kindness and benevolence as well as through courage.

bushido Literally, the "Way of the Warrior." Bushido is the samurai philosophy, a loosely defined system of values and concepts sometimes honored, sometimes not, during Japan's feudal period.

bushi no nasake (the tenderness of the warrior) The refinement, grace, and tenderness expected of the samurai of old Japan.

chudan kamae (middle level posture) A stance taken with the sword held directly in front of the body, pointing toward an opponent's throat. This is the basic posture for training in swordsmanship.

chuden (middle level teaching) The intermediate level techniques of a school of martial art.

daimyo The provincial lords of feudal Japan. Many were also military leaders.

deai (initial moment of moving together) The initiatory action of the martial artist in combat. To move swiftly from absolute stillness is the aim of deai training.

dojo (place for learning the way) Originally a term for a Buddhist temple, the dojo is a training hall for the bugei or budo. The behavior of the trainee in the dojo is customarily one of reverence and respect.

Fudo Shinmyo Roku ("Record of Immovable Wisdom") A treatise on the relationship between swordsmanship and Zen, written in the form of a letter by the priest Soho Takuan to Yagyu Munenori during the latter half of the sixteenth century.

fukuro shinai A mock sword, made of a wood or bamboo core and padded with leather or cloth. The fukuro shinai is used sometimes in fencing practice so blows may be landed against an opponent safely.

go The oldest board game in the world. Go was invented in ancient China, but refined to a high state of sophistication in feudal Japan. The intent of go is to capture territory and some of an opponent's playing pieces. Because it is basically military in nature, go was played by martial artists as a means of learning strategy.

hakama A pleated, skirt-like pair of pants, usually black or white, worn by practitioners of the classical martial disciplines. (They were worn by the samurai as a form of everyday dress.) Students of aikido and kyudo (archery) also wear hakama during training.

hara The region about two inches below the navel that is the focal point of balance. It is also, according to traditional Japanese thought, a person's spiritual center. It was for this reason that samurai wishing to kill themselves chose the method of hara-kiri (see *seppuku*), literally opening their hara for examination.

heiho The strategies and philosophy of a ryu.

Heihokadensho ("A Chronicle of Strategy") A treatise written by Yagyu Munenori, outlining the strategy of the Yagyu school of the martial arts.

hoben (secret methods or teachings) The word comes from Buddhism and is frequently given to martial arts techniques, the principles of which are customarily not revealed to those outside the ryu.

Hozoin The Hozoin was a Buddhist temple more famous for the fighting abilities of its monks than for its piety. The Hozoin clergy were experts in a style of spearmanship named after their temple, the Hozoin ryu.

iaido/iaijutsu The art of drawing a sword quickly and striking. Iaijutsu is part of the curriculum of most traditional ryu. Typically it consists of three components, nukitsuke (drawing), kiri (cutting), and noto (returning the blade to the scabbard). Iaijutsu is practiced from standing and sitting postures and was studied by the classical swordsman so that he could defend himself with his sword in any situation. Iaido is the modern budo form of iaijutsu, practiced as an exercise in grace and mental composure.

iaigoshi A crouching posture of readiness, from which the sheathed sword can be drawn in an instant. The swordsman often sat in iaigoshi to be in a favorable position to defend himself against a surprise attack.

jingasa A shallow, bowl-shaped helmet, worn by the samurai in battle. Stylized versions of the jingasa served as the family crest (mon) of the Yagyu clan.

jutsu (art) Meaning an art or craft, this word is also used as a suffix. For example, the art, jutsu, of the blade, ken, is kenjutsu, the art of fencing.

Kage ryu Literally meaning "shadow style," the Kage ryu was one of the older ryu of swordsmanship in Japan. The name refers to the "shadow" or mental intent of an opponent, which was discerned by the skilled exponent of the Kage ryu before an attack was physically begun. Aizu Hyuga no kami Iko is credited with formally establishing the ryu, c. 1500.

kaishaku The assistant in the ceremony of seppuku. The kaishaku was responsible for decapitating the rite's performer after the initial cut was self-inflicted. Kaishaku had to be highly proficient swordsmen to carry out their terrible job correctly.

kamae Any of the postures taken during martial arts training or performance. Kamae in the classical bugei were extremely specialized and it was possible to determine an opponent's school and ability merely by observing his kamae.

kami Often translated as "gods," kami are better thought of as spirits. In the Shinto faith many objects, including rocks, trees, and mountains are all thought to be imbued with spirits. These are their kami. In common speech, kami is also used to mean "upper" or "above."

kamiza (spirit seat) A special shrine erected at the front of the dojo to honor the spirits and ancestors of the ryu. The kamiza is the spiritual center of the dojo.

kanji The calligraphic characters that make up the Japanese system of writing. Kanji can also be written with a creative flair, as an artistic form.

Kashima ryu A school of the art of Japanese fencing. It influenced many other later ryu and was allegedly founded by the famous swordsman Tsukahara Bokuden in the early sixteenth century.

kata A ritualized series of movements designed to simulate actual combat, thus providing the martial artist the opportunity to polish his abilities. The kata often have secret meanings and applications other than those seen by the uninitiated. Their significance is found as much in training the mind to respond quickly and fluidly as it is in the practice of technique. The kata are the very heart of a ryu, the means by which a school's traditions and strategies are handed down through successive generations. Modern exponents who would eschew kata in favor of more "realistic" means of training miss the entire point of these movements and effectively remove themselves from serious pursuit of the martial arts.

katana The Japanese sword.

katsujinken (the sword that takes life)   A teaching of the Yagyu ryu, referring to a swordsman who wields his weapon to end life. The warrior with this kind of sword is the lowest form of martial artist. (See *satsujinken*)

kendo (sword way)   The modern budo form of traditional swordsmanship. Kendo uses the flexible shinai, made of bamboo, rather than a bokken or real sword. Its goals are more character development and sport than self protection (upon which the older kenjutsu is based). Many Japanese today confuse kendo with its predecessor, kenjutsu, but the two actually have little in common and provide a good example of the contrast between the budo and the bugei or bujutsu.

kenjutsu (sword art)   The classical art of swordsmanship, kenjutsu is divided into a myriad of ryu, all with distinctive methods, techniques, and strategies, and all rooted in the age of feudalism, when swordsmanship was of practical value. Today kenjutsu is maintained for its historical value and as a means of preserving the cultural ethics of the Japanese warrior.

kenshi A master swordsman.

kenshin ittai (sword and mind as one)   The concept of making the sword move in perfect harmony with the mind and body of the swordsman. This relationship is a primary goal of kenjutsu training.

ki The animating force of life, according to Japanese thought.

kime The focus of power in an attack or block. The proper application of strength, speed, and shock, all delivered at exactly the right moment, produces kime.

Kinki A region of northern Nara Prefecture, marked by steep mountains and small, isolated villages. The hamlet of Yagyumura is located in the Kinki district.

kisagake A whipping action of the sword as it is removed from the scabbard quickly in an attack, meant to cut through an opponent.

Kojiki ("Record of Ancient Matters") A book, part religion and part folktale, containing the epic myths of the founding of prehistoric Japan.

Koyagyu The villa of the Yagyu family, located on a hill above the village of Yagyumura, in present day Nara Prefecture. Only the foundation of the building remains today.

kumi-uchi Unarmed grappling methods of the samurai. This early form of jujutsu was employed on the battlefield when weapons were unavailable.

misogi The ritualized "cleansing" of spirit and body, stemming from Shinto practices. Misogi often involves standing under waterfalls or submersion in lakes and rivers, but it is also used to mean all sorts of austere disciplines spiritual in nature. A popular form of misogi for martial artists calls for seated meditation and chanting for long periods of time.

mushin (without mind) The state of consciousness where the body responds naturally, without undue interference from the mind. Movements and reactions that are spontaneously correct are said to be the result of mushin, which is achieved only after a period of strenuous training and effort in some form of Zen.

muto (without sword)   The muto are the unarmed techniques of the Yagyu ryu, employed to disarm an attacker who is wielding a sword. Many of the muto techniques of the Yagyu school were studied by the founder of modern aikido, Morihei Uyeshiba, who incorporated them into his budo.

naginata A long polearm, resembling a halberd. The naginata was used with wide sweeping motions designed to take advantage of its lengthy blade and haft. Several bugei ryu included a study of the naginata in their curriculum.

nakaima The idea in Japanese thought that current generations are one link in the continuing chain of human existence. According to the principles of nakaima, to be grateful for the efforts of previous generations is best demonstrated by being responsible for the well-being of those that will follow.

ninja Practitioners of the art of ninjutsu, the craft of assassination, terrorism, and espionage in feudal Japan. There were two varieties of ninja: samurai who specialized in ninjutsu (a part of many bugei ryu), and the more common variety, ordinary criminals hired for their unsavory services. The "secret agent/commando" exploits of the ninja have been grossly sensationalized. In historical reality, the ninja played a mysterious political role in the establishment of many feudal dynasties, an area of Japanese history that remains little explored.

obi A belt or waist wrapping. In kenjutsu, the obi is a long strip of cloth, worn under the hakama, into which the sword scabbard is thrust to facilitate carrying it.

okuden (hidden teaching)   Also known as okugi, these are the secret teachings or techniques of a ryu. Often the okuden involved principles based upon magic or esoteric religion.

okugi (hidden methods)   (See *okuden.*)

ronin (wave man)   A samurai without a master or lord to serve. The ronin are usually pictured as romantic figures in Japanese fiction, wandering the length of the country and engaging in all sorts of adventures. Actually, many were forced to earn a living through banditry.

ryu   A school or style of the martial arts or ways, characterized by its own particular teaching methods, strategies, techniques, and traditions. Many of the classical bugei ryu are interconnected or have a number of offshoot ryu founded by various masters of the original. For example, teachings of the original Kage ryu were modified and improved, giving birth to the Shinkage ryu. Later, this ryu was adapted by the Yagyu masters, to become the Yagyu Shinkage ryu, which in turn was later divided into many derivative schools, among them the Owari Yagyu Shinkage, Edo Yagyu Shinkage, and Yagyu Shingan.

sageo   A cord or sash connected to the scabbard of a Japanese sword, usually tied to the swordsman's belt or waist to secure the weapon when worn on the hip.

sama   A polite form of address, added as a suffix to someone's name. The use of sama was more common during the feudal era in Japan than it is now.

samurai   The warrior class of feudal Japan, also known as the bushi.

satsujinken ("the sword that spares life")　A concept of the Yagyu ryu indicating that the aim of the swordsman should be in preserving life and protecting it, rather than in taking it. This was the opposite of katsujinken, the sword used only for killing. The ideal of satsujinken versus katsujinken is considered one of the first steps taken by classical bugeisha to elevate their arts into more philosophically-oriented martial ways.

saya　The scabbard of a Japanese sword, usually made of wood.

seigan kamae　A version of the chudan, or middle level posture in fencing, in which the sword is held in an aggressive manner, with the tip threatening an opponent's eyes.

seishi choetsu　To overcome fears of life or death.

seishin tanren (spirit forging)　To strengthen the spirit through difficult training in the martial arts or ways.

seiza　A seated position used by the Japanese, who customarily sat on the matted floors of their homes. In seiza, the knees are folded back so that one is sitting on his crossed ankles.

sensei (teacher)　Literally, the word means "one who has come before." It does not necessarily mean a master (*hanshi*) or a role model, but a guide to one's own development.

seppuku　Ritual suicide by disembowelment. This is the more proper way of saying "hara-kiri."

settsuku　Literally, "connection." Settsuku in the martial arts refers to the connection between all parts of the body when moving to attack or defend oneself.

shibumi The aesthetic quality of severe simplicity. Shibumi is quiet, graceful, and hidden beauty, usually found in an everyday object, or in nature.

shinai The mock sword used in modern kendo. The shinai is made of strips of bamboo bound together. Its shape and weight are very different from that of a real sword, leading many traditional swordsmen to disapprove of its use, primarily sporting, in kendo.

Shinkage ryu "New Shadow school." The swordsmanship of the Kage ryu was refined by Kamiizumi Nobutsuna in the late sixteenth century to become his Shinkage style. The Shinkage ryu was the parent school of the Yagyu Shinkage ryu.

shinobi-nin Another name for the ninja.

Shinto The native religion of Japan. Shinto is actually a form of animism and nature worship in which a variety of natural objects are believed to be imbued with deities. (See *kami*.) Shinto places emphasis on ritual cleanliness and purification of the spirit to achieve harmony with others and oneself.

shiseido (the way of femininity)　The attributes of feminine grace and beauty, esteemed in traditional Japanese culture.

shoden (first level)　The fundamental techniques of a ryu.

shogun The military ruler of Japan. The title was first bestowed on Minamoto Yoritomo in 1192. It was claimed by various generals, most notably those of the clan of Tokugawa, until the abolishment of feudalism in 1867.

sohei Warrior priests. The sohei typically in-habited mountain monasteries. They were brave and skillful warriors, whose military and political activities were an important influence on the history of early Japan.

sojutsu The art of the Japanese spear.

sometsuke An official of the Tokugawa government who was responsible for gathering military and domestic information. In this sense, the sometsuke could be thought of as a spymaster. Yagyu Mitsuyoshi Jubei, the third headmaster of the Edo Yagyu Shinkage ryu, was a sometsuke for the Tokugawa shogunate.

tachi-ai The standing posture of readiness the swordsman takes in preparation for drawing his weapon.

tameshigiri (test cutting) A corollary art of swordsmanship that requires the exponent to test his cutting technique against different targets. These include dampened straw wrapped into lengths, columns of bamboo, and, in the feudal age, human beings, dead and alive.

tengu Goblins, or mountain sprites of Japanese folk myths. The tengu, according to legend, were brilliant martial artists, and many ryu trace their beginnings to a founder's meeting with them. Tengu were allegedly the reincarnation of vain Buddhist priests.

Tomita ryu A very old school of swordsmanship in Japan, probably founded by Tomita Kuroemon, in the early fifteenth century.

tomoe karasu (circling crows) A principle of combat of the Yagyu Shinkage ryu. The tomoe karasu are techniques that involve deflecting or avoiding an opponent's strike by moving in the path of a circle. The movement is likened in form to the shape of a flock of crows rising in a winding flight above a field. For this reason, crows are often depicted as ornaments on weaponry and armor used by swordsmen of the Yagyu Shinkage style.

waza A technique.

Yagyumura The home village of the Yagyu clan. Yagyumura is northeast of the city of Nara, in present day Nara Prefecture. It is the site of the Hotoku Temple, where records of the Yagyu family and their ryu are still kept.

Yagyu Shinkage ryu A school of swordsmanship, founded by Yagyu Munenori during the fifteenth century. The Yagyu school of the sword is notable because its masters served as instructors to most of the Tokugawa shoguns and because of its link to the discipline of Zen. The original Yagyu school eventually split into several offshoots, including the Edo and Owari Yagyu Shinkage. All are referred to as the Yagyu Shinkage ryu, or simply the Yagyu ryu.

yari The Japanese spear.

zanshin (remaining mind) The spirit of alertness and concentration that pervades the actions of the master in the martial arts.

Illustrations

A Note on the Crests

The family crests, or *mon*, of the Yagyu clan are representations of a *kasa*, a broad-brimmed hat designed to keep rain, snow, and sun out of the wearer's face. Originally worn by women working in the fields, the kasa was eventually adopted by travellers and others in feudal Japan who were outdoors frequently. One version of it became popular with ladies of the nobility, and another, the lacquered *jingasa*, became a favorite headgear of the samurai. Like Western heraldry, family crests in Japan were handed down by parents to their children. They were used to decorate clothing and other personal possessions, serving also as a form of legal identification, much as a signature or seal does today. Therefore, the mon of a son was altered in some way to distinguish it from his father's or brother's. Often these changes were slight. The mon of the offspring of Yagyu Munenori, for example, can be discerned by variations in the tassels of the kasa's connecting cords.

Succeeding generations of the Yagyu line varied the mon further to identify themselves, and they shared the kasa motif with another samurai family, the Takebe of Harima Province, but it remains a distinctive symbol of the great clan of master swordsmen from Yamato, the Yagyu.

 The mon of the Matsunaga family, allies and retainers of the Yagyu, is one of the maple leaf variety, a motif used by other well-known warrior clans, including the Takayama, the Imadegawa, and the Ichikawa. Specifically, the Matsunaga mon is the *akigetsu ni nozoki kaede*, or "Maple Leaf Peeking Under an Autumn Moon." Originally the round "moon" in the crest was light and the leaf darker colored, but sometime in the sixteenth century the colors were reversed by the head of the family's main branch, and it has remained so ever since.

Notes on the Illustrations of Sword Guards (tsuba), *which appear throughout the book.*
These *tsuba* were all designed and cast by Yagyu Renyasai Toshikane (1625-1694), the fourth headmaster of the Yagyu Shinkage ryu.

Renyasai wrote the *Sanjuroku Kasen*, or *Thirty-Six Poets*, which is comprised of thirty-six aphorisms containing many of the principles of the Yagyu school in their messages. Some of these he symbolically incorporated in his guards. Renyasai was actually more famous as a craftsman-artist than he was as a swordsman. The tsuba originally appeared in *Sukashi Tsuba-Bushito no Bi*, by Masayuki Sasano.
Title and dedication:
Both these tsuba are depicting the *kazeho*, or "wind filled sail." The image of a ship traveling across the waves is fundamental to Yagyu strategy, which equates the mind to a ship. The ship cuts through the water on its journey, leaving nothing but a quickly disappearing wake behind it. So too, thought Yagyu Munenori, should be

the swordsman's attitude in combat, constantly flowing with the action, not stopping on any one thing.

Foreword, preface, chapter 1:

All three are *Suigetsu*, "The Moon and Water." This is another analogy found in Yagyu *heiho*. As long as the water is placid, it reflects perfectly the image of the moon. But if it's ruffled, the moon's reflection is shattered. As long as the swordsman keeps himself in a state of tranquillity, he can see the intentions of others, but if he allows himself to become agitated, the reflection is scattered.

Chapter 2:

Nobuteranami, "Waves of Sunlight through the Waves." The waves, no matter how they rage, cannot resist the passage of sunlight through them, nor can the sunlight, no matter how bright, cause the waves to cease their motion. This has to do with accepting fate as it is. There's an expression in Japanese that means rather much the same thing: the mountain doesn't make fun of the river for being lowly, and the river doesn't give the mountain a hard time about not being able to get about.

Chapter 3:

Nami ni kai, "Waves and an Oar." The waves here represent life's vicissitudes; the oar is our morality, knowledge, and desires, which attempt to steer us successfully through the life's sea. Notice, in the upper right-hand corner, a wild goose. The goose represents the spiritual aspects of the scenario, removed from the everyday facets of our voyage, but catching our attention from time to time.

Chapter 4:

A *tori* or Shinto shrine gate, with waves (*Nami-torii*). In the opening part of his classic work on Yagyu *heiho*, Munenori compared entering the way of swordsmanship to entering a gate—passing across a threshold to a new way of thinking and living.

Chapters 5 and 6:

Tatsunami, "Waves and Water Droplets" and *Marunami*, "Circling or Breaking Waves," are two themes representing the fluidity of combat. This fluidity is also applied to daily life.

Chapter 7:

A *Take-kiribaku*, or "bamboo stump" design. The bamboo figured prevalently in Japanese thought, representing the ability to bend before the inevitable so that one can survive to bounce back again. Renyasai also included a stylized depiction of the bamboo's roots. See the foreword for the reason behind this analogy: to remember and strengthen our own roots.

Chapter 8:

Waniguchi, "Shrine Gong." When a bell's rung, the sound stays on in the air, in a kind of resonance. We don't have a word for it, but the Japanese do. They call that *yoin*. It has long been a part of the aesthetical sense of seeing—or in this case, hearing—subtleties. Renyasai admired the swordsman who was so highly refined that he could appreciate this kind of thing.

Chapter 9:

Tobi karasu, "Circling Crows." This is a beautiful tsuba, relating directly to a Yagyu combat strategy. When an opponent attacked, the swordsman moved in a circle, whirling like a flock of crows taking off from a field, slipping past the attacker's force. This guard is a reminder of that movement.

Chapter 10:

Kiku, "Chrysanthemum." This tsuba is purely decorative.

Chapter 11:

Another decorative tsuba, of the Diamond or *Hishi* style. Renyasai may not have had any symbolism in mind here. He may have been making a reference to the *Diamond Light Sutra* of Shingon Buddhism. The little hearts on the top and bottom, by the way, aren't early evidence of St. Valentine's appearance in the land of the rising sun. In Japan, this shape is called *Inoshishi no me,* "the wild boar's eye."

Chapter 12:

Sansei-sankaku, "Three Stars in a Triangle." One posture assumed by practitioners of aikido is called *sankaku-dai*. This posture is taken from the Yagyu school of fencing, and is the meaning in this guard, one of dynamic balance within stillness.

Afterword:

Saihai ni horagai. A military commander's baton and conch shell trumpet.

Glossary:

Hechimadana, "Sponge Gourd and Trellis." Another purely decorative tsuba.

Sources of the Illustrations

Half-title page:
Autumn Lightning
Calligraphy by Iwakura Yoshinori.
Page 1:
Yagyu Shinkage Ryu
Calligraphy by a Yagyu swordsman.
Chapter 2:
Katsujinken, satsujinken.
Calligraphy by a Yagyu swordsman.
Chapter 4 through Afterword:
Courtesy of the village of Yagyu.